Healthy food isn't going to do anyone any good if no one is eating it—it has to taste great!

—Elaine Magee

Fry Light, Fry Right

Fry Light, Fry Right

Fried-Food Flavor Without Deep Frying
Delicious, crispy "fried" foods that are good for you!

by Elaine Magee, MPH, RD

Black Dog & Leventhal
Paperbacks

Published by

Black Dog & Leventhal Publishers
151 West 19th Street
New York, NY 10011

Distributed by

Workman Publishing Company
708 Broadway
New York, NY 10003

Manufactured in China

Cover and interior design by 27.12 Design, Ltd.

ISBN: 1-57912-391-0

g f e d c b a

Library of Congress Cataloging-in-Publication Data on file at
Black Dog & Leventhal Publishers, Inc.

DEDICATION

This book is for my two girls, Devon and Lauren. It is hard for me to imagine that you both will be in college within five to seven years—it truly does go too fast. Being your mother is the most important thing that I do and I wouldn't trade our time together for anything in the world. One of my "mother" goals was for me to really know who you are and for you both to really know who I am. I think we've done that.

Thank you both for understanding when I have book deadlines and countless recipes to test. No matter how crazy our lives get, we all have our love for each other (and Daddy) to hold on to. I feel so totally blessed and grateful that you are in my life.

Table of Contents

Confessions of a Dietitian Who Loves Fried Foods

I admit it! Not including chocolate (which is ranked number one), some of my favorite foods are deep fried. Tempura, apple fritters, funnel cakes, fried chicken, french fries—shall I keep going? You get the picture. I'm a dietitian who loves fried foods. And to top it off, I even have the type of irritable bowel syndrome (IBS) that doesn't fare so well when greasy foods enter the picture. The answer? **Fry Light, Fry Right** foods.

I've been officially lightening up recipes for twenty years now, and over those years, I've learned a few tricks where fried foods are concerned. I've been able to rescue a number of prized dishes that I'd threatened to banish from the dinner table. I still make foods like eggplant Parmesan, chimichangas, and egg rolls—I just make them with a lot less oil. Does it ruin these favorite foods to make them the light way? I'm sure some people would say it does. But everyone else is pleasantly surprised when they taste a healthy version of a favorite fried food that has the same delicious flavor and texture but is nice and light in the stomach, too.

The need to lighten up foods may be more urgent for some of us than others, particularly those who, like me, have a medical condition that makes eating deep-fried foods an uncomfortable situation. Been there and done that more times than I can count! I know firsthand what a dose of greasy food can do to you before you even leave the restaurant. In the United States alone, more than 25 million people suffer from some degree of IBS, so I know I'm not alone. And more than 15 million Americans suffer from heartburn daily (a major symptom of acid reflux), and there are an additional 45 million who have heartburn at least once a month. So there are many, many people (including some type 2 diabetics) for whom fried foods are on the "don't go there" list.

So if our diets are restricted, what can we eat instead? I think a large portion of us who are motivated to eat healthily—whether for personal or medical reasons—quite simply want more than poached chicken breasts and steamed vegetables. We crave the fried foods we grew up with and that continue to tempt us at restaurants and fast-food establishments. The answer is not to binge on these forbidden foods when we just can't stand it anymore, only to feel sick—emotionally and physically—almost immediately afterward. If instead we turn to some new methods, which require little more than a bit of oil and a hot oven or pan, we can have our fried foods and eat them, too.

Compared to deep-frying, foods fried in the oven or pan in a minimum of oil have countless health benefits. I also contend that they're often tastier, more convenient, and less likely to cause discomfort in people who suffer from IBS or acid reflux (or other medical conditions where greasy, high-fat foods can cause big problems). Not only that, but there's no worry about where to put all the used oil. When you make these recipes, there isn't any used oil to get rid off; there isn't even anything to drain off. Every bit of oil called for is needed by the food. And there's another bonus—your house isn't going to end up smelling like the corn dog stand at a carnival. For those of us who don't have the biggest and best kitchen fan,

there's something about heating a small vat of oil that causes this odor to permeate the entire house.

But it isn't just the grown-ups who benefit from **Fry Light, Fry Right** foods. Most kids adore fried foods, and the techniques used in this cookbook make many kid-cuisine standouts more healthful. Without all the extra calories and fat grams from deep-frying, children actually reap the benefits of the food itself, be it the antioxidants and fiber of potatoes, or the protein, vitamin B12, and iron from chicken breast.

With few exceptions, anything that deep-frying can do, the oven or nonstick frying pan can do, too. And if you can eat a lighter version of a favorite fried food that tastes just as good, why wouldn't you? I hope you'll try some of the recipes in this cookbook. It is my wish that you will love these light dishes as much as I do and that you will become a **Fry Light, Fry Right** believer, too!

CHAPTER 1

Why Do Fried Foods Taste So Good?

WHY DO FRIED FOODS TASTE SO GOOD?

Think, for a moment, about the foods Americans adore—foods that epitomize Americana. My guess is about half are deep-fried in a vat of fat. Take your pick: french fries, potato chips, doughnuts, southern-fried chicken, chicken nuggets, corn dogs. It has even become a bona fide culinary trend to deep-fry a Thanksgiving turkey! And many of our favorite ethnic foods, such as egg rolls and wontons, flautas and taco shells, tempura and falafel, are deep-fried as well.

DO YOU KNOW YOUR "FRIED FOODS" HISTORY?

Exactly when did America begin its love affair with deep-fried foods anyway? "We know that before Columbus's time, there was no deep-frying," notes Barbara Haber, curator of books at the Schlesinger Library at Harvard University. Since Native Americans traditionally didn't deep-fry, this technique of cooking foods was, in part, imported to America along with its immigrants. According to Haber, part of the reason people around the world started deep-fat frying comes from wanting (and needing) to use every part of the animal . . . including the fatty parts. "It wasn't just a choice to fry foods—up until the 1800s, people didn't have the option of home ovens, they were mostly cooking over an open flame," adds Haber.

So now that we all have ovens conveniently located in our home kitchens, why is America still deep-frying food? "We fry foods today for two main reasons," explains Charles Perry, food historian and staff writer in the food section of the **Los Angeles Times.** "Fat tastes good and it's quick and easy compared to warming up an oven then baking." It's true—deep-frying is definitely faster. It isn't a coincidence that most fast food is fried. For example, it takes exactly five to seven minutes to deep-fry a basket of french fries. If you bake them instead, you'll need about 25 minutes (not including the time it takes to preheat the oven). But does deep-fat-fried food actually taste better?

When you deep-fry foods, you get not only quick cooking time but two other appealing results as well: an appetizing golden brown color with a rich flavor, and a crispy exterior with a moist interior. That sounds pretty hard to beat, doesn't it? "I've always loved deep-fried food," says Sharon Tyler Herbst, author of **The New Food Lover's Companion**. Sharon confesses that for people like her who grew up with these foods, eating them today is the ultimate indulgence. "If we can have that look, taste, and crunch of deep-fried food without all the calories and fat, it would be the best of both worlds," she adds. Well, Sharon, the **Fry Light, Fry Right** foods come darn close to making this wish come true!

YOU CAN HAVE YOUR FRIED FOODS AND EAT LIGHT, TOO!

After twenty years of lightening recipes, I've found (with a few exceptions) that anything a deep-fat fryer can do, an oven or nonstick frying pan can do just as well—and sometimes even better. Many of the desirable characteristics of deep-fried foods can be duplicated in your oven or in your nonstick frying pan with a little bit of oil. Of course, it isn't quite as simple as shaking and baking. You still need to coat the food with some fat, albeit a much smaller amount, in order to get some browning and

crisping on the surface. And depending on the food being oven- or pan-fried, you might also need to add a cooking technique or two to the recipe to pull it off (such as thickening the batter with some extra flour or broiling the food for a minute or two at the last to create a crunchy brown exterior).

Achieving that absolutely addicting "crispy on the outside" and "moist on the inside" eating experience is what the eight light-frying techniques in chapter 3 aim to do (see page 33). If you're willing to try these light-frying techniques and add a few more minutes to your prep time, you can have your cake and eat it, too. Rather, you can have your fried chicken and french fries and eat light, too!

IT'S ALL IN THE CRUNCH

Texture contrast is a big part of what makes fried foods so much fun to eat. Whether it's mozzarella sticks or beef flautas, you can get the same effect with oven or nonstick pan "frying." The foods in this cookbook, freed from immersion in bubbling baths of oil, are often coated with breading, then sprayed or lightly brushed with canola or olive oil, and cooked crisp in a very hot oven or over high heat. This method of light "frying" lets the cook know exactly how much oil is absorbed, whereas with deep-fat frying, that's a difficult thing to measure. Some foods can literally soak up the oil like a dry sponge. Just to prove this, I've performed what I call "the disappearing oil trick" on numerous occasions, measuring the oil both before and after frying. Each time I was shocked to see how much oil the food absorbed. Whatever oil was missing from the pan when I removed the fried food . . . this was the amount that was now literally sitting on and in the food itself.

THE FLAVOR BOOST OF BROWNING IS HARD TO BEAT

The other major reason deep-fried foods are so irresistible is that the hot-fat bath causes the browning and caramelization of natural sugars and starches in the food. It is no coincidence that the breading or batters that cloak food before it's fried generally contain a starch and/or some sugar. But here's a news flash— you don't need to deep-fry foods in unlimited amounts of oil to get caramelization and browning to take place. You only need to lightly coat the outside of the food with little droplets of oil to get the process started.

Browning in general brings out amazing flavors; just think of a nicely browned sirloin steak. And have you ever tried tasting those "browned bits" that are left over after you pan-fry chicken or meat? They're full of intense, yummy flavors, which is why we often flavor our gravies and sauces with them. Keep in mind that this "toasting" of starches and sugars generally requires fairly high temperatures, while moist and moderate cooking methods such as boiling and steaming don't reach high enough temperatures to brown foods. But broiling, baking, and frying do—and all three are covered in this cookbook.

DOES FAT TASTE GOOD?

All of the discussion thus far leads us to the million-calorie question: Since deliciously brown and crispy fried foods are cooked in fat, does fat taste good? Most of us would answer, Of course. But it isn't fat molecules per se that we actually taste when we think we're "tasting" the fat in food. Fat molecules are actually too big to be processed by the taste buds. What we really experience are three things:

- The impurities and volatiles that mix with fats, such as with high-flavor oils like olive and sesame, or bacon, or my personal favorites—butter and chocolate. (Volatiles in food may be released in the high-temperature frying process.)

- The smells in fat. Fat is a solvent for smells that eventually make their way to the nasal receptors. Therefore, in many cases, the greater the amount of fat, the greater the "smellability" of particular flavors.

- The unique flavors that caramelization contributes.

All of which is good news. It means that when we cook the **Fry Light, Fry Right** way, we can still sense the flavors of caramelization, enjoy the crunch of "fried" foods, and smell the volatiles and impurities in fat. Why? Because we are still using fat in many of the recipes—we're just limiting ourselves to the magical minimum necessary to crisp up and cook the food.

THE BROWNING BENEFIT

Browning food and caramelizing its natural sugars brings out rich, desirable flavors. Here are just a few examples:

- Browned butter has a much more intense and rich taste than chilled butter.

- Roasted marshmallows have a deeper, more addictive taste than regular marshmallows.

- Heating sugar to a light or dark brown color (as is the case when making toffee) brings out a whole new range of wonderful flavors.

- Toasted or roasted nuts taste better than raw nuts. When you toast nuts in a pan or oven, you can literally smell their flavor increasing as they start to turn golden brown. Raw nuts, on the other hand, don't smell like anything in particular.

CHAPTER 2

Why Are Deep-Fried Foods So Bad For Us?

WHY ARE DEEP-FRIED FOODS SO BAD FOR US?

Excess calories and fat grams . . . that's basically what it comes down to. Deep-fried foods tend to be higher in fat grams and therefore higher in calories than the same foods prepared another way.

To illustrate the difference deep-frying makes, let's take a look at chicken, fish, and potatoes:

• **Chicken:** A roasted skinless chicken breast has approximately 142 calories and 3 grams of fat. A breaded and fried chicken breast, with skin on, has about 364 calories and 18.5 grams of fat. Just for fun, let's compare two types of fast-food chicken sandwich options—the grilled chicken breast sandwich at McDonald's (Chicken McGrill Sandwich), with its typical toppings, contains 400 calories and 16 grams of fat; the Crispy Chicken Sandwich, on the other hand, has 510 calories and 26 grams of fat.

• **Fish:** Deep-frying has a similar effect on fish. A serving (3.5 ounces, or 100 grams) of baked cod at Long John Silver's contains 120 calories, 4.5 grams of fat, and 1 gram of saturated fat. A piece (3.2 ounces, or 92 grams) of fried fish at the same restaurant contains 230 calories, 13 grams fat, and 4 grams saturated fat. Pretty amazing, isn't it?

• **Potato:** Last but not least, let's see what happens to our favorite "veggie." A large baked potato (7 ounces, or 202 grams) contains approximately 220 calories and 0.2 gram of fat. That same baked potato turned into french fries contains 697 calories and 34 grams of fat. Wow!

We could keep going over example after example, but the bottom line is still the same. **When you fry foods, you add calories and fat grams.**

FAT: THE GOOD, THE BAD, AND THE UGLY

Why are fried foods bad for you? It's not just because they quickly add excess fat grams and calories to your daily totals—often leading to "excess" on the body as well. It's also what the foods are fried in that becomes a concern. If foods are cooked in fat that contains trans fats (trans-fatty acids) such as shortening and partially hydrogenated oil, or saturated fats such as butter, lard, bacon grease, and coconut or palm kernel oil, then the amount of fat is even more worrying; these types of fats are

FACE TO FACE WITH FRYING

The term "frying" can apply to a number of different cooking techniques. Here are some definitions to help you sort things out:

- DEEP-FRY: To cook food in hot fat that is deep enough to completely cover the item being fried.

- SAUTÉ: To fry in a small amount of fat. (In many recipes, though, even sautéing can lead to higher calories and more fat grams. So in this book, I've lightened up some recipes that are normally sautéed in a large amount of fat.)

- STIR-FRY: To fry quickly over high heat in a lightly oiled pan while stirring continuously. (I've found, however, that some stir-fry recipes call for quite a bit of oil. Actually only a small amount is needed to produce crisp, tender food.)

strongly linked to an increased risk of heart disease and possibly other health problems as well, including type 2 diabetes and some forms of cancer. (See the sidebar The Trouble with Trans and Sat Fats for more information on these evildoers.) Health experts may not agree on quite a few dietary matters, but most agree that a decreased intake of saturated fat (less than 10 percent calories from saturated fat) and trans-fatty acids (as little as possible) is imperative. Saturated fat is listed on the nutrition information label of food products; we should start seeing trans fats listed in 2005.

This means trans fats are most likely hiding in the following foods:

- Most margarines and shortenings, which can contain 20 to 40 percent trans-fatty acids

- Frying fats used in industrial food preparation

- Deep-fried fast food, including french fries

- Crackers listing partially hydrogenated oils in the ingredients

- Cake mixes and frostings listing partially hydrogenated oils in the ingredients

- Snack cakes listing partially hydrogenated oils in the ingredients

- Packaged snack foods listing partially hydrogenated oils in the ingredients

- Chips listing partially hydrogenated oils in the ingredients

- Doughnuts listing partially hydrogenated oils in the ingredients

- Piecrusts listing partially hydrogenated oils in the ingredients

- Biscuits listing partially hydrogenated oils in the ingredients

- Breakfast cereals listing partially hydrogenated oils in the ingredients

- Frozen waffles listing partially hydrogenated oils in the ingredients

- Microwave popcorn listing partially hydrogenated oils in the ingredients

- Packaged cookies listing partially hydrogenated oils in the ingredients

- Other baked and fried items containing partially hydrogenated vegetable oils

Anything with animal fat, hydrogenated oil, palm kernel oil, palm oil, or coconut oil is going to contain saturated fat. So higher-fat animal foods such as butter, whole-milk dairy, and higher-fat meats are high in saturated fat; food products like higher-fat crackers, cookies, snack cakes, and chips contain higher amounts of trans fats.

The big trouble is that many commercially prepared fried foods contain saturated and trans fats. But when you fry your foods at home, you can use a vegetable oil that's low in saturated fat and higher in the better fat—monounsaturated fat (highest in canola oil and olive oil)—as well as the possibly protective polyunsaturated fat, or plant omega-3 fatty acids (also found in canola oil).

CHOOSE YOUR OILS CAREFULLY

We know that to cook foods the healthy way, we can use "better" oils such as olive and canola, which are both rich in the preferred monounsaturated fat; canola oil also contains some omega-3 fatty acids (from plants). But are all good-for-you oils good for frying, too? Not quite. The oil or fat used in high-temperature frying must have a "high

THE TROUBLE WITH TRANS SAT FATS

When you think of "bad fats" in terms of health effects, saturated fats usually come to mind. Well, they've got company. Health-wise, the effects of trans-fatty acids are akin to those of their bad-boy sat-fat brother—except trans fats offer a double whammy to your blood lipid profile. In addition to raising your "bad cholesterol" (LDL) levels, the way saturated fat does, trans fats decrease your "good cholesterol" (HDL) levels at the same time.* This is one of the reasons many researchers consider trans fats to be a bigger threat than saturated fat.

Trans-fatty acids are unsaturated fatty acids that contain at least one double bond in the "trans" configuration. They occur naturally at low levels in meat and dairy products, and they are formed during a process called "partial hydrogenation" of vegetable oils. This process transforms some of the oil's unsaturated fat into trans-fatty acids, which makes them more solid and stable. Over the years, food manufacturers have used partially hydrogenated oils in their products to improve their texture and shelf life. Most of the trans fat in North American diets comes from these partially hydrogenated fats and oils.

But don't let the dangers of trans fats distract you from the importance of also reducing saturated fats in your daily diet. Americans eat far more saturated fat than trans fat, so reducing both fats is vital to our health.

*Arteriosclerosis Thrombosis Vascular Biology 21:7 (July 2001), 1233–7.

WORDS FOR THE WISE

TRANS-FATTY ACIDS are formed during hydrogenation of oils, a process used by food manufacturers to make these oils (and the foods made from them) more solid and long lasting—ideal qualities for life on the supermarket shelf. The partial hydrogenation process results in a large percentage of molecules called trans-fatty acids. Most of the fat in American diets comes from these manufactured trans fats, rather than from the very small amounts that occur in the milk of cows and sheep.

HYDROGENATED AND PARTIALLY HYDROGENATED FATS have been chemically altered (made more saturated and therefore more solid) by the addition of hydrogen atoms. If a vegetable oil is completely saturated or "hydrogenated," it becomes a saturated fat. When a vegetable oil is partially hydrogenated, some trans-fatty acids are formed. Margarine and shortening are examples of products that are made with partially hydrogenated and hydrogenated fats.

SATURATED FATS are fatty acids that have the maximum possible number of hydrogen atoms attached to every carbon atom. These fats are "saturated," or "full" of hydrogen atoms. Saturated fats are found in large amounts in animal fats (especially butter, lard, beef, pork, lamb, and whole-milk dairy products; less so in poultry and fish). Plants have little saturated fat, except coconut and palm oils, which are known as "tropical oils."

LIPOPROTEINS are chemical compounds made of fat and protein. Lipoproteins that have more fat than protein are called low-density lipoproteins (LDLs)—also known as "bad" cholesterol. Lipoproteins that have more protein than fat are called high-density lipoproteins (HDLs)—known as "good" cholesterol. Lipoproteins are found mainly in the blood, where their main function is to carry cholesterol around. A high level of LDL cholesterol in the blood increases the risk of fatty deposits forming in the arteries, in turn increasing the risk of heart attack. Elevated levels of HDL cholesterol, on the other hand, seem to have a protective effect against heart disease.

smoke point," the point to which the oil can be heated without smoking or breaking down. The reason shortening and lard are commonly used in frying is that both have high smoke points. But never fear—there are some vegetable oils with low sat fats and trans-fatty acids that also have higher smoke points, and they can be used to fry food just as easily. (Remember that even though in this cookbook we are using just a little oil to oven- and pan-fry, we still need high smoke points because we are cooking at high temperatures.)

Which are the best oils to use in **Fry Light, Fry Right** recipes? We need to use something with higher monounsaturated fat, which brings us to olive oil and canola oil. And it would be nice if the oil also contributed some of those beneficial plant omega-3 fatty acids. Lastly, our oil should have a high smoke point so it can handle the temperatures we'll be using to pan-fry, bake, and broil our dishes. Of the two oils that contain the highest levels of monounsaturated fat, only one has omega-3 fatty acids and a high smoke point—canola oil. So canola oil's our go-to guy for frying. But I still use olive oil in some recipes that don't require heating (such as a dip or spread) or that call for more moderate cooking temperatures.

THE OUTRAGEOUS OIL MYTH

Have you heard this one? Some proponents of deep-frying profess that if the temperature of the fat is hot enough, the food will be crispy on the outside and moist on the inside without absorbing much fat at all. I'm not buying this, are you? If there were a magical temperature for frying oil that produced healthy foods, wouldn't that be reflected in the nutrition contents of our favorite fast foods? Then why are these various fried fast-food items so high in calories and fat?

• Carl's Jr. Onion Rings (one side order) = 436 calories, 22 grams fat, 5 grams saturated fat

• Three "Crispy Strips" Chicken Strips from KFC = 400 calories, 24 grams fat, 5 grams saturated fat

• Carl's Jr. Fried Zucchini (one side order) = 318 calories, 19 grams fat, 5 grams saturated fat

- Long John Silver's Battered Shrimp (eight pieces; about 110 grams, or 4 ounces) = 340 calories, 22 grams fat, 7 grams saturated fat

FRIED FOOD "BEFORE AND AFTERS"

Yes, we've debunked the myth of healthy deep-fat frying, but that doesn't mean we can't enjoy the taste and texture of our favorite fried foods. Give them a nutritional makeover, and with few exceptions we've got to-die-for oven- and pan-fried foods that won't kill us. Take a look at the "before" and "after" nutritional profiles of some of the fried foods featured in this cookbook:

EXAMPLE #1—CHICKEN NUGGETS

In my opinion, the best-tasting fast-food chicken nuggets are the all-white-meat version from Wendy's. They taste pretty good, but aren't very good for you. Let's compare them with the oven-fried, all-breast chicken nuggets in this cookbook:

- **5 WENDY'S CRISPY CHICKEN NUGGETS**
  220 calories
  14 grams fat
  3 grams saturated fat
  13 grams carbohydrates
  11 grams protein

- **5 OVEN-FRIED CHICKEN BREAST NUGGETS**
  191 calories
  4.3 grams fat
  0.6 gram saturated fat
  8 grams carbohydrate
  28 grams protein

SAVINGS About 30 calories and 10 grams of fat per serving!

EXAMPLE #2—GARLIC FRIES

When I go to the ballpark to watch a baseball game, I am mesmerized by the smell of Garlic Fries (a specialty of my home team stadium). But . . . the fries are deep-fried, and then a garlic butter sauce is drizzled over the top. I've come to love the light version I make at my home kitchen "stadium" with oven-fried potatoes and a lighter garlic sauce. Check out the difference this makes in the calorie and fat department:

- **BALLPARK GARLIC FRIES**
  490 calories
  28 grams fat
  10 grams saturated fat
  56 grams carbohydrate
  4 grams protein

- **OVEN-FRIED GARLIC FRIES**
  256 calories

7.7 grams fat

3.3 grams saturated fat

42.3 grams carbohydrate

5.9 grams protein

SAVINGS About 230 calories and 20 grams of fat per serving!

EXAMPLE #3—COCONUT SHRIMP

Coconut Shrimp is a popular appetizer in many restaurants across the country. It's all about shrimp being battered, rolled in coconut, and then deep-fried until golden. We are still battering the shrimp (in a lighter batter), and rolling in coconut, but then we're coating them lightly with canola cooking spray and baking in the oven until golden. Just as yummy but a whole lot lighter:

- **DEEP-FRIED COCONUT SHRIMP**

    377 calories

    20.6 grams fat

    5.4 grams saturated fat (or more)

    16 grams carbohydrate

    31 grams protein

- **OVEN-BAKED COCONUT SHRIMP WITH FRESH PINEAPPLE SALSA**

    257 calories

    7 grams fat

    4.7 grams saturated fat

16 grams carbohydrate

31 grams protein

SAVINGS 120 calories and almost 14 grams fat per serving!

See the difference? Much better, don't you think? But as I always say, healthy food isn't going to do anyone any good if no one is eating it. It has to taste good. That's why I test my lightened recipes on all sorts of people—and the recipes in this book were very well-liked across the board. Remember in the preface where I admitted to loving fried foods? Well, it's because I love fried foods that I can be a pretty tough critic myself. I can't wait to make all sorts of these recipes again—the Corn Fritters, the Oven-Fried Artichoke Hearts, the Veggie Tempura, the Apple Fritters, the Mango Chimichangas, the entire appetizer chapter . . . don't get me started!

In the next chapter, I'll clearly outline the **Fry Light, Fry Right** cooking techniques so you can see just how easy they are. After that it's on to the actual recipes!

CHAPTER 3

Flawless Frying
(with Less Fat)

Can we really make over our favorite fried foods into lighter, better-for-us dishes? For most of our favorite fried foods—yes, we can! I'll warn you up front: It will take a little more time to oven-fry the food (pan-frying in a lot less fat takes about the same amount of time as deep-frying, though). But that's a small price to pay for cutting the calories and fat as much as we do.

Before working on this book, I'd already had some success transforming deep-fried foods into light and tasty, oven-fried or pan-fried versions (which is what gave me the idea for this cookbook). But I had no idea, 120 recipes later, that the lightening techniques I started with would work so well with so many different types of fried foods—from regional favorites like corn fritters and fish tacos, to fun finger foods like jalapeño poppers and buffalo wings, to popular entrées like eggplant Parmesan and coconut shrimp, to ethnic favorites like chicken flautas and tempura, to all sorts of fast foods and desserts. I know it's hard to believe, but almost anything that's traditionally coated in crumbs—chicken nuggets, fish sticks, crab cakes, what have you—can easily be oven-fried, often with the same crumb mixture. And even

food that is coated in batter can successfully be fried in a nonstick skillet or the oven with a lot less oil. Admittedly, the battered food can be a bit trickier to lighten because the batter has to stand up to a longer cooking time in the oven without literally slipping off the food. But I've found a way to make it work.

Deep-fried egg rolls and spring rolls, and deep-fried yeast dough (like doughnuts), were probably the most difficult fried foods to work on. In my experience, the oven can't reproduce the bubbling of the egg roll and spring roll wrappers that takes place when they are dunked in hot oil, and it can't create the same raised doughnut texture and exterior when yeast doughnut dough is fried. But with a little tweaking of the traditional recipes, I was able to figure out how to make wrappers almost as crispy as they should be, and yeast dough rise nearly like it normally does. You'll see how in the following techniques.

FLAWLESS FRY LIGHT, FRY RIGHT TECHNIQUES

These are the eight techniques I used to create tasty, lower-fat versions of our favorite fried foods that emphasize the more healthful fats whenever possible.

Please also keep in mind one rule of thumb: In order to mimic effects of hot deep-fat frying, the oven or nonstick frying pan must be hot enough to brown the food and seal in the juices (but not so hot that it burns).

1. Use a small amount of canola oil to coat the surface of the food, then brown in a 400° F (200° C) oven or a nonstick frying pan over high or medium-high heat instead of deep-fat frying in a bath of oil.
2. Add moisture to meat first by marinating in buttermilk or other low-fat liquids. After you have tenderized the meat, you can coat it with crumbs or batter and continue with the oven- or pan-frying technique described in #1.
3. Give yeast breads that are traditionally fried, such as doughnuts, time to rise on their own (in traditional preparations, these breads rise during the deep-frying process). Coat the outside with canola cooking spray and brown in the oven.
4. Batters offer a bit of a challenge, but there are two options for success. First, you can thicken the batter by adding a starch ingredient (or less liquid) so it stands up better to the longer cooking times of oven-frying. Second, you can replace a traditional recipe's wet batter with a dry crumb coating, or add a crumb coating to the outside of the batter. Crumb coatings generally oven- and pan-fry very well.
5. Instead of creating a crispy crust by deep-frying food in hot oil, add crispy ingredients to the outside of the food before oven-frying.
6. Broil foods toward the end of oven-frying to quickly add color and crisp texture to the outside of the food.
7. For some deep-fried foods that use a batter, you can brown the battered food item very nicely in a nonstick skillet or frying pan by coating the food or the pan lightly with canola oil and cooking over high heat.
8. What little cooking fat you use should be higher in plant omega-3 fatty acids and/or monounsaturated fats whenever possible. Olive oil works well in recipes that aren't cooked at the higher (around 400° F, or 200° C) temperatures (and where the olive flavor is favorable); canola oil works well in all pan- and oven-frying situations since it has a neutral taste and handles high temperatures well.

NOT JUST ANY OIL WILL DO

Even though we're using a lot less oil in these **Fry Light, Fry Right** recipes, the choice of oil is still an important one. It's pretty obvious as you flip through the recipes that canola oil is my overwhelming first choice. Canola oil is expressed from rapeseeds and is the most widely used oil in Canada. Here are the top five reasons why canola oil is one of your best oil choices:

- Canola oil is the lowest in 'saturated fat of the vegetable oils, with 6 percent saturated fat (peanut oil, for example, is 18 percent saturated fat).

- Canola oil is the second highest in the preferred monounsaturated fats (the first being olive oil—but as we know, olive oil does not have a high enough smoke point for oven-frying).

- Canola oil is the vegetable oil highest in plant omega-3 fatty acids (omega-3 fatty acids are thought to lower cholesterol and triglycerides and provide many other possible health benefits).

- Canola oil has a neutral flavor that doesn't compete with the natural flavors of the food being fried.

- Canola oil is reasonably priced and widely available.

Some recipes in this book will call for measurements of oil straight out of the bottle, but many call for cooking spray. With so many options at the supermarket, finding the "right" spray can be daunting. My suggestion is to buy a spray that is specifically made from canola oil, and also one made from olive oil, if you'd like. One of the many advantages of cooking spray is that it disperses very small droplets of oil over a certain pan or dish or food, which means you can easily coat foods with bumpy or curved surfaces and use less oil than you would with regular oil.

You may be wondering how a product such as cooking spray, in which the main ingredient is oil, can be calorie- and fat-free. Well, it's not entirely. A one-second spray of cooking oil can add up to 7 calories and 0.7 gram of fat. But this is far less than the 122 calories and 13.6 grams of fat found in a tablespoon of oil. In certain recipes in this book, when I generously coat...the food with canola cooking spray, I accounted for this fat in the nutritional analysis.

There's also another option if you're bothered by the thought of throwing away several cans of cooking spray a year. You can try the Misto brand oil sprayer or others like it, which you fill yourself (with your desired oil) and pump manually before spraying. If you choose this option, make sure to clean the sprayer regularly and store it in a cool place in the kitchen.

A BIT ABOUT BALANCE

Before I send you off to begin enjoying all the **Fry Light, Fry Right** foods in this cookbook, I want to go over a few healthy eating recommendations. If your goal is to eat a healthy diet to protect yourself from as many diseases as possible, it isn't quite enough just to switch to eating **Fry Light, Fry Right** foods instead of deep-fried foods (although it's a great start). It's also vital that you eat plenty of fruits and vegetables (strive for at least five servings a day altogether), whole grains whenever possible, beans and legumes more often, and fish a couple of times a week.

Switching to lower-fat dairy products, leaner and smaller portions of meat, and skinless poultry, as well as reducing the use of saturated fat and trans fats in cooking, is also a good idea. Eating this way should keep your fiber and vitamin/mineral/antioxidant levels high, too!

You've heard the term "balanced meals"? Well, most bodies tend to fare better with meals or snacks that are balanced—that contribute a little protein and fat along with some carbohydrate. Eating a variety of foods means that our energy is more likely to stay even, we're more likely to get recommended levels of various nutrients, and we're more likely to feel full and satisfied. Keep this in mind when preparing the recipes in this book. There's no need to get crazy about it; just use some common (nutritional) sense. You could serve the Spicy Chicken Tenders in chapter 6, for example, with a nice green salad, some fruit, and maybe a whole grain. And the only companionship the Light Eggplant Parmesan in chapter 5 needs is some steamed broccoli and a big melon wedge. The best part is that you can enjoy the **Fry Light, Fry Right** recipes without worrying about what you're eating. All of the major nutritional values are listed after each recipe, so you'll always know what to expect. If you're keeping track of your nutritional intake—counting carbs, fat grams, and fiber because you are diabetic, or sodium because of high blood pressure, or simply watching calories or tallying omega-3 fatty acids—you're in luck. You can easily fit these foods into a balanced, healthy, wholesome diet, because by and large they are healthy and wholesome, too.

Now, let's get cooking!

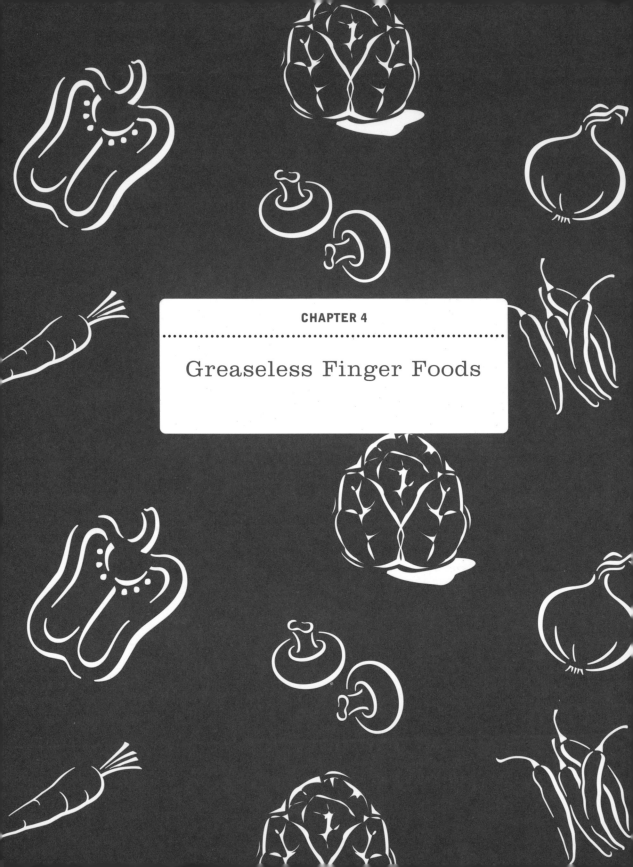

CHAPTER 4

Greaseless Finger Foods

Oven-Fried Artichoke Hearts in Garlic-Herb Batter

MAKES 5 SERVINGS (about 4 quartered artichoke hearts per serving)

This is one of the regional recipes that comes from my neck of the country! You can find deep-fried artichoke hearts at the Santa Cruz Beach Boardwalk (Northern California), or the Garlic Festival (Gilroy, California), or at a few restaurants and Italian delis. I fashioned this recipe after my memories of the artichoke hearts I used to look forward to in Santa Cruz—they were battered in an herb batter, then deep-fried. For this light version, I whipped up a lighter batter and pan-fried the artichokes in a little bit of oil.

2 6-oz. (170 g) jars marinated artichoke hearts, drained (reserve 1/4 c. juice*) (about 1 1/3 c. drained artichoke hearts)

2 tbsp. egg substitute (such as Egg Beaters)

1/2 tsp. ground black pepper

3/4 tsp. Italian herb blend

3/4 tsp. minced garlic

6 tbsp. Reduced Fat Bisquick pancake mix

1 tbsp. canola oil

Shredded or grated Parmesan cheese (optional)

Finely chopped fresh parsley (optional)

1. Combine the artichoke hearts, artichoke heart juice, egg substitute, pepper, herb blend, and minced garlic in a medium-sized bowl. Gently stir in the pancake mix to make a nice batter.
2. Heat the canola oil in large, nonstick frying pan over medium-high heat.
3. Spoon the artichokes, one at a time, into the hot pan using a slotted spoon, making sure there's enough batter surrounding the artichoke hearts to coat them nicely. Fry until golden brown on the bottom, then flip over and brown the other side (about 3 minutes a side).
4. Top the hot artichoke hearts with a sprinkling of Parmesan cheese and fresh, finely chopped parsley if desired. Serve immediately.
* NOTE: If you are using marinated artichoke hearts that have oil in the marinade, you can spoon off the top layer of oil, then use a basting bulb to siphon off the juice from the bottom of the jar.

NUTRITIONAL ANALYSES (PER SERVING)

	BEFORE	AFTER		BEFORE	AFTER
CALORIES	180	84	CHOLESTEROL	42 MG	0 MG
PROTEIN	3.5 G	3 G	FIBER	3 G	3 G
CARBOHYDRATES	11.5 G	11.5 G	SODIUM	161 MG	159 MG
FAT	14 G	3 G	% CALORIES FROM FAT	70	32
SATURATED FAT	1.9 G	0.3 G	OMEGA-3 FATTY ACIDS	0.4 G	0.3 G
MONOUNSATURATED FAT	4.7 G	1.7 G	OMEGA-6 FATTY ACIDS	7 G	0.6 G
POLYUNSATURATED FAT	7.4 G	0.9 G			

Jalapeño Chili Poppers

MAKES 12 POPPERS

If you have declined store-bought or restaurant jalapeño poppers in the past because they tend to be too hot (or unhealthy) for you, you'll love these! This deliciously light, mildly spicy recipe uses bottled jalapeño chilies that are drained well and have the fiery seeds removed. Yum!

1 16-oz. (454 g) jar jalapeño peppers
("tamed" jalapeños are also available)
4–5 oz. (110–140 g) reduced-fat sharp
cheddar or Montcrey Jack cheese
1/2 c. egg substitute (such as Egg Beaters)
2 tbsp. Wondra quick-mixing flour

2/3 c. plain fine breadcrumbs
(French breadcrumbs if available)
3/4 tsp. garlic powder
1/2 tsp. salt
1/4 tsp. paprika
Canola cooking spray

1. Preheat the oven to 400° F (200° C).
2. Drain the jalapeños well. Remove about 1/4 inch of the tip of each pepper. Use the handle of a small spoon to remove and discard the seeds of each jalapeño. Dry on paper towels.
3. Cut the cheese into thin strips and stuff each jalapeño with as much cheese as possible.
4. Add the egg substitute to a bowl, sprinkle the Wondra over the top, and stir with a fork until smooth.
5. Add the breadcrumbs, garlic powder, salt, and paprika to a small, shallow bowl. Stir with a fork to blend well.
6. Holding a pepper by the stem, dunk it into the thickened egg mixture, then into the breadcrumb mixture to coat well. Repeat. Still holding the pepper by the stem, coat the outside well with canola cooking spray and place on a cookie sheet. Be sure the peppers do not touch or they won't crisp up as well.
7. Repeat with the remaining peppers. Bake until peppers are lightly browned, about 18 minutes. Remove from the oven and serve immediately.

NUTRITIONAL ANALYSES (PER POPPER)

	BEFORE	AFTER		BEFORE	AFTER
CALORIES	99	54	CHOLESTEROL	32 MG	7 MG
PROTEIN	4 G	4 G	FIBER	0.3 G	0.3 G
CARBOHYDRATES	4 G	4 G	SODIUM	239 MG	239 MG
FAT	7.6 G	2.4 G	% CALORIES FROM FAT	69	40
SATURATED FAT	2.9 G	1.5 G	OMEGA-3 FATTY ACIDS	0.1 G	0 G
MONOUNSATURATED FAT	2.1 G	0.5 G	OMEGA-6 FATTY ACIDS	2.1 G	0.1 G
POLYUNSATURATED FAT	2.2 G	0.1 G			

Savory Stuffed Mushrooms

MAKES 6 SERVINGS

Searching for the ultimate stuffed mushroom recipe, I made two different versions before trying this one. One taste and the search was over. A savory reduced-fat cream cheese mixture fills each baby portobello mushroom, which is then dipped in a thickened egg substitute mixture before being coated in breadcrumbs. The outside of each mushroom is coated with canola cooking spray and baked in a hot oven.

6 whole baby portobello mushrooms
    (or large porcini or button mushrooms,
    if you're in a pinch)
1 tsp. canola oil
1 1/2 tsp. minced garlic
2 tsp. white wine or nonalcoholic beer
1/2 c. light cream cheese
3 tbsp. grated Parmesan cheese
2 pinches ground black pepper

2 green onions, finely chopped
    (white and part of green)
1/8 tsp. ground cayenne pepper
1/4 c. egg substitute
    (such as Egg Beaters)
1 1/2 tbsp. Wondra quick-mixing flour
2/3 c. plain breadcrumbs (use French
    breadcrumbs if available)
Canola cooking spray

1. Preheat the oven to 450° F (230° C). Line a baking sheet with aluminum foil. Clean the mushrooms with a damp paper towel and carefully break off the stems. Remove and discard the tough ends of the stems and finely chop the remaining stems (you will have about 1/3 cup).
2. Heat the canola oil in a medium, nonstick saucepan or frying pan over medium heat. Add the garlic, chopped mushroom stems, and wine or beer. Fry until any moisture has disappeared (but be careful not to burn the garlic), about 3 minutes. Remove from the heat and let the mixture cool for about 5 minutes.
3. Stir the cream cheese, Parmesan cheese, black pepper, green onions, and cayenne pepper into the mushroom mixture (or blend together using a small food processor or electric mixer). Using a small spoon, completely fill each mushroom cap with the cream cheese mixture.

4. Place the egg substitute in a small bowl. Sprinkle the Wondra flour over the top and stir with a fork until smooth. Place the breadcrumbs in a separate small bowl.
5. Dip each mushroom, cap-side down, first in the egg substitute mixture (dip up to the top edge of the mushroom—do not dip the filling into the egg), and then in breadcrumbs to coat the outside of the mushroom. Spray the outsides of the mushrooms with canola cooking spray. Place the mushrooms cap-side down onto the prepared baking sheet.
6. Bake for about 30–35 minutes or until the cream cheese filling is nice and bubbly and the mushrooms are cooked through. Serve immediately.

NUTRITIONAL ANALYSES (PER SERVING)

	BEFORE	AFTER		BEFORE	AFTER
CALORIES	166	91	CHOLESTEROL	59 MG	9 MG
PROTEIN	5 G	7 G	FIBER	0.5 G	1 G
CARBOHYDRATES	7 G	8 G	SODIUM	180 MG	181 MG
FAT	13.5 G	3.5 G	% CALORIES FROM FAT	73	34
SATURATED FAT	6 G	1.5 G	OMEGA-3 FATTY ACIDS	0.2 G	0.1 G
MONOUNSATURATED FAT	3.5 G	0.7 G	OMEGA-6 FATTY ACIDS	3 G	0.2 G
POLYUNSATURATED FAT	3.5 G	0.3 G			

Garden Veggie Egg Rolls
with **Two Sauces**

MAKES 12 EGG ROLLS

When I first developed these tangy egg rolls, they were so good I found myself eating the leftovers cold from the refrigerator the next day! The veggie-filled egg roll wrappers are placed on a cookie sheet that has been coated with a small amount of canola oil, and rolled around to coat the outside. They are then baked in the oven and broiled at the end to help brown the exterior. I suggest serving these with either Orange Hoisin Sauce or Mango Ginger Sauce (recipes follow)—or both!

1 recipe Orange Hoisin Sauce or
    Mango Ginger Sauce
4 tsp. canola oil, divided
2 tsp. minced or chopped garlic
1 c. firm tofu, diced into 1/2-inch cubes
2 c. finely shredded Napa cabbage
1 c. bean sprouts

1/2 c. finely chopped celery
1/3 c. chopped green onions
    (white and green sections)
1/2 c. grated carrot
12 egg roll wrappers (found in produce
    section of most supermarkets)
1 egg, beaten

1. Preheat the oven to 400° F (200° C). Spread 2 teaspoons of canola oil evenly over a small cookie sheet (add a teaspoon more if needed). Prepare the dipping sauce(s).
2. Add the remaining 2 teaspoons of canola oil to a large nonstick frying pan or skillet over medium-high heat. Add the garlic and tofu and cook for about 2 minutes, stirring frequently. Add the cabbage, bean sprouts, celery, green onions, and grated carrot; continue to cook, stirring, for 2 more minutes. Remove from the heat and set aside to cool.
3. Stack the wrappers on a clean work area and cover with a damp cloth. Lay one wrapper on a flat surface, one corner facing you, and spoon 1/4 cup of filling about 2 inches from the bottom corner. Shape the filling horizontally into a long sausage shape and drizzle with 1/2 tablespoon of the Orange Hoisin Sauce or Ginger Mango Sauce.

4. Fold the bottom corner over the filling and roll upward one turn so the filling is completely encased. Moisten the left and right corners of the triangle with the beaten egg, fold in the corners, and press down firmly to seal, creating an envelope. Moisten the top corner of the skin with beaten egg and give one more turn, sealing the cylinder.

5. Place the egg roll on the prepared sheet and roll it around to lightly coat the exterior with oil.

6. Repeat steps 3 through 5 with the remaining filling and wrappers. Bake for 15 minutes in the center of the oven. Flip over and bake for 8–10 minutes more.

7. Transfer the egg rolls to the broiler, about 6 inches from the flame, and broil until brown and crispy. Remove from the oven and serve with the remaining sauce for dipping.

NUTRITIONAL ANALYSES (PER EGG ROLL)

	BEFORE	AFTER		BEFORE	AFTER
CALORIES	101	78	CHOLESTEROL	30 MG	1 MG
PROTEIN	3 G	3 G	FIBER	1.1 G	1.1 G
CARBOHYDRATE	10 G	12 G	SODIUM	274 MG	102 MG
FAT	6 G	2.3 G	CALORIES FROM FAT:	53	26
SATURATED FAT	1.2 G	0.2 G	OMEGA-3 FATTY ACIDS	0 G	0.2 G
MONOUNSATURATED FAT	2.9 G	1.1 G	OMEGA-6 FATTY ACIDS	1.3 G	0.6 G
POLYUNSATURATED FAT	1.3 G	0.8 G			

Orange Hoisin Sauce

MAKES 3/4 C.

1/2 c. bottled hoisin sauce (available in the Asian foods aisle of your supermarket)

3 tbsp. orange juice

1 tbsp. rice vinegar

2 tsp. grated orange zest

1 1/2 tsp. minced garlic

2 tsp. minced peeled fresh ginger

Place ingredients in a small bowl and stir well. (Can be made 1 week ahead and stored in a covered container in the refrigerator.)

FRY LIGHT, FRY RIGHT PREPARATION (PER TBSP.)*

CALORIES	27	FIBER	0.4 G
PROTEIN	0.4 G	SODIUM	172 MG
CARBOHYDRATE	6 G	% CALORIES FROM FAT	13
FAT	0.4 G	OMEGA-3 FATTY ACIDS	0.02 G
SATURATED FAT	0.06 G	OMEGA-6 FATTY ACIDS	0.16 G
MONOUNSATURATED FAT	0.1 G		
POLYUNSATURATED FAT	0.2 G	*Nutritional analysis does not differ significantly	
CHOLESTEROL	0.3 MG	from traditional preparation.	

Mango Ginger Sauce

MAKES 3/4 C.

1 mango (about 1 1/4 c. chopped,
    peeled, pitted, and diced mango)
1 tbsp. honey

1 tsp. lime juice
1/2 tsp. chopped fresh ginger

Place the ingredients in a small food processor and puree until smooth.
Cover and refrigerate up to 3 to 5 days.

FRY LIGHT, FRY RIGHT PREPARATION (PER TBSP.)*

CALORIES	17	OMEGA-3 FATTY ACIDS	0 G
PROTEIN	0.1 G	OMEGA-6 FATTY ACIDS	0 G
CARBOHYDRATES	4 G		
FAT	0 G	*Nutritional analysis does not differ significantly from
CHOLESTEROL	0 MG	traditional preparation.
FIBER	0.3 G		
SODIUM	0.4 MG		
% CALORIES FROM FAT	0		

Avocado Egg Rolls
MAKES 8 EGG ROLLS

Avocado Egg Rolls are one of the most popular menu items at a very popular restaurant chain, The Cheesecake Factory. These are their oven-fried cousins. If you can't find fresh cilantro in your grocery store, fresh basil can be substituted. These taste good all by themselves, but you could dip them in warm jalapeño jelly, salsa, nonfat sour cream, or the Fresh Pineapple Salsa on page 89.

2 tsp. canola oil
2 c. diced avocados (about 2 avocados)
3 tbsp. chopped sun-dried tomatoes (can use bottled julienned sun-dried tomatoes, drained and chopped)
1/4 c. finely chopped red onion
1/4 c. finely chopped fresh cilantro (loosely packed)
Salt and pepper to taste
8 large square egg roll wrappers (such as Azumaya brand)
Warm water, for sealing edges

1. Preheat the oven to 450° F (230° C). Coat a 9- x 13-inch baking dish with 2 teaspoons of canola oil and set aside.
2. Place the diced avocados, sun-dried tomatoes, red onion, and cilantro in a medium-sized bowl and toss to mix well. Add salt and pepper to taste.
3. Stack the wrappers on a clean work area and cover with a damp cloth. Lay one wrapper on a flat surface, one corner facing you, and spoon 1/4 cup of filling about 2 inches from the bottom corner. Shape the filling horizontally into a long sausage shape.
4. Fold the bottom corner over the filling and roll upward one turn so the filling is completely encased. Moisten the left and right corners of the triangle with warm water, fold in the corners, and press down firmly to seal, creating an envelope. Moisten the top corner of the skin with warm water and give one more turn, sealing the cylinder.
5. Place the egg roll in the prepared dish and roll it around in the oil to lightly coat the exterior.
6. Repeat steps 3 through 5 with the remaining filling and wrappers. Bake until nicely browned and crisp, about 18–20 minutes.

NUTRITIONAL ANALYSES (PER EGG ROLL)

	BEFORE	AFTER		BEFORE	AFTER
CALORIES	188	122	CHOLESTEROL	1 MG	1 MG
PROTEIN	3 G	3 G	FIBER	2.5 G	2.5 G
CARBOHYDRATES	13 G	13 G	SODIUM	122 MG	122 MG
FAT	13.8 G	7 G	% CALORIES FROM FAT	66	51
SATURATED FAT	1.9 G	1 G	OMEGA-3 FATTY ACIDS	0.2 G	0.2 G
MONOUNSATURATED FAT	5.9 G	4.3 G	OMEGA-6 FATTY ACIDS	5 G	1 G
POLYUNSATURATED FAT	5.2 G	1.2 G			

Eggplant Bruschetta Bites

MAKES AT LEAST 12 SERVINGS

This recipe takes beloved bruschetta to a whole new level. This is not only a fun finger food, but actually counts toward a vegetable serving.

1 tbsp. olive oil or canola oil
1 egg (a higher omega-3 egg if available)
1/4 c. egg substitute
   (such as Egg Beaters)
2 tbsp. water
1 1/2 c. plain dry breadcrumbs

1 large eggplant, ends cut off and then
   cut into 1/4- to 1/2-inch round slices (at
   least 12 slices)
Canola or olive oil cooking spray
About 2 c. bottled brushcetta sauce or
   marinara sauce
1/2 c. shredded or grated Parmesan cheese

1. Preheat the oven to 375° F (190° C). Spread the bottom of a jelly roll pan with olive oil or canola oil.
2. In medium-sized bowl, whisk the egg and egg substitute with 2 tablespoons of water. Place the breadcrumbs in a separate medium-sized, shallow bowl. Dip each eggplant slice, one by one, into the egg mixture, then in the breadcrumbs, and then place them on the prepared jelly roll pan. You should be able to fit 12 of the rounds on one jelly roll pan.
3. Coat the tops of the eggplant with canola or olive oil cooking spray. Top the slices evenly with the sauce and Parmesan cheese.
4. Bake in the oven for about 20 minutes, then transfer to the broiler and continue cooking for 3 to 5 minutes (watching carefully so the eggplant does not burn) more, until lightly golden and the cheese is bubbling. Cool slightly before serving.

NUTRITIONAL ANALYSES (PER SERVING)

	BEFORE	AFTER		BEFORE	AFTER
CALORIES	141	83	CHOLESTEROL	75 MG	11 MG
PROTEIN	4.4 G	3.5 G	FIBER	2 G	2 G
CARBOHYDRATES	11.1 G	11 G	SODIUM	244 MG	240 MG
FAT	9.1 G	3 G	% CALORIES FROM FAT	58	31
SATURATED FAT	1.9 G	0.8 G	OMEGA-3 FATTY ACIDS	0.07 G	0.03 G
MONOUNSATURATED FAT	3 G	1.3 G	OMEGA-6 FATTY ACIDS	3 G	0.15 G
POLYUNSATURATED FAT	3.1 G	0.2 G			

Veggie Samosas

MAKES 22 SAMOSAS

This is my vegetarian rendition of a recipe for Seven-Spiced Beef Samosas (see page 72). The traditional beef recipe already included some vegetables (potatoes, peas, and onions), so I've added red bell pepper and carrots to replace the beef and complement the other flavors. For this lighter version, I had to change the shape a bit from the traditional triangle to more of a cylindrical egg roll—it's the best way to get the phyllo dough crispy all over. Plan ahead if you're using frozen dough, which must thaw for five hours at room temperature or overnight in the refrigerator.

4 c. potato cubes (about 2 large potatoes, peeled and cut into 1/2-inch cubes)
1 c. fresh or frozen peas
1 c. finely chopped onion
1 c. finely diced red bell pepper
1 c. finely diced carrot
4 tsp. minced or chopped garlic
1 tbsp. minced fresh gingerroot (1 tsp. ground)
1/2 tsp. ground black pepper
1 tsp. salt
1/2 tsp. ground cumin

1/2 tsp. ground coriander
1/2 tsp. ground turmeric
1/2 tsp. chili powder
1/2 tsp. ground cinnamon
1/2 tsp. ground cardamom
2 tbsp. chopped fresh cilantro
2 tbsp. chopped seeded fresh green chili peppers (canned are okay, if necessary)
1 16-oz. (454 g) package phyllo dough, refrigerated or frozen (see headnote)
Canola cooking oil
1 tbsp. canola oil (optional)

1. Bring a medium saucepan of lightly salted water to a boil. Stir in the potatoes and peas. Cook until the potatoes are tender but still firm, about 15 minutes. Drain, mash together, and set aside. (You can also microwave the potatoes and peas on high in a covered dish until the potatoes are tender, about 18 minutes.)
2. In a large nonstick saucepan over medium-high heat, heat the onions, red bell peppers, and carrots. Cook until the mixture is evenly brown and the onions are soft, about 5 minutes. Mix in the garlic, fresh gingerroot, and dry seasonings. Stir in the mashed potato mixture. Remove from the heat and chill in the refrigerator for 1 hour, or until cool.

3. Preheat the oven to 450° F (230° C). Mix the cilantro and green chili peppers into the potato mixture.
4. Remove the phyllo dough from the package and place it under a sheet of waxed paper; cover with a damp towel. Lay a single sheet of phyllo dough out on a clean, flat surface and fold it in half widthwise (when folded, the sheet should be almost square). Place approximately 1/4 cup of filling in a lengthwise sausage shape in the center; fold over the short sides and one long side. Roll up to create a 3- to 4-inch-long cylinder, and seal the edges by pressing the dough together with water-moistened fingers.
5. Place the veggic samosas on a nonstick baking sheet that has been well coated with canola cooking spray. Coat the top of the samosas with the spray or lightly brush with some canola oil. Bake for about 20–30 minutes or until golden brown. Serve immediately.

NUTRITIONAL ANALYSES (PER SAMOSA)

	BEFORE	AFTER		BEFORE	AFTER
CALORIES	147	107	CHOLESTEROL	0 MG	0 MG
PROTEIN	3 G	3 G	FIBER	2 G	2 G
CARBOHYDRATE	22 G	22 G	SODIUM	228 MG	228 MG
FAT	5 G	0.5 G	% CALORIES FROM FAT	31	4
SATURATED FAT	0.6 G	0 G	OMEGA-3 FATTY ACIDS	0.1 G	0.1 G
MONOUNSATURATED FAT	1.2 G	0.1 G	OMEGA-6 FATTY ACIDS	2.8 G	0.2 G
POLYUNSATURATED FAT	3 G	0.3 G			

Potato Skins with Quick Ranch Dip

MAKES 8 POTATO SKINS

These potato skins are healthy and delicious. If you'd like, you can save the scooped-out potato for mashed potatoes tomorrow.

4 medium russet potatoes, scrubbed, baked or microwaved, then cooled slightly

About 2 tsp. canola oil

1/2 c. grated reduced-fat sharp cheddar or Monterey Jack cheese

4 strips Louis Rich turkey bacon, cooked until crisp and crumbled into pieces

2 green onions, trimmed and finely chopped

Freshly ground pepper (optional)

1. Preheat the oven to 450° F (230° C). Line a thick cookie sheet with foil.
2. Cut the potatoes in half lengthwise. Scoop out most of the inside, leaving about 1/4 inch of potato attached to the skin.
3. Brush the inside and skin side of each potato half lightly with canola oil, and set it on the prepared pan skin-side down. Bake in the preheated oven for about 10 minutes, until lightly brown.
4. Place the grated cheese, crumbled bacon, and green onions in a small bowl and toss to blend. Sprinkle evenly over the potatoes (be careful to get the filling in and on the potatoes, not the cookie sheet). Top with freshly ground pepper if desired.
5. Bake until the cheese is bubbly, about 8 minutes.
6. Set the potato skins on a serving dish and serve with Quick Ranch Dip (opposite) or light sour cream.

NUTRITIONAL ANALYSES (PER TBSP, NOT INCLUDING QUICK RANCH DIP)

	BEFORE	AFTER		BEFORE	AFTER
CALORIES	180	123	CHOLESTEROL	13 MG	11 MG
PROTEIN	5 G	5 G	FIBER	1.3 G	1.3 G
CARBOHYDRATES	22 G	17 G	SODIUM	156 MG	156 MG
FAT	8.5 G	4 G	% CALORIES FROM FAT	43	29
SATURATED FAT	3 G	1.5 G	OMEGA-3 FATTY ACIDS	0.1 G	0.1 G
MONOUNSATURATED FAT	2.5 G	1.2 G	OMEGA-6 FATTY ACIDS	2.9 G	0.7 G
POLYUNSATURATED FAT	3 G	0.7 G			

Quick Ranch Dip

MAKES ABOUT 1/2 C.

1/2 tbsp. Hidden Valley Ranch dip mix   2 tsp. light or low-fat mayo
1/2 c. fat-free or light sour cream   (or 1 tsp. regular mayonnaise*)

Combine the ingredients in a small bowl and mix until smooth. Serve immediately or store in the refrigerator for several days until needed.

FRY LIGHT, FRY RIGHT PREPARATION (PER TBSP.)**

	BEFORE	AFTER		BEFORE	AFTER
CALORIES	75	19	SODIUM	120 MG	21 MG
PROTEIN	8 G	0.8 G	% CALORIES FROM FAT	96	28
CARBOHYDRATES	0.5 G	2.5 G	OMEGA-3 FATTY ACIDS	N/A	0 G
FAT	8 G	0.6 G	OMEGA-6 FATTY ACIDS	N/A	0.2 G
SATURATED FAT	1.3 G	0.2 G			
MONOUNSATURATED FAT	N/A	0.2 G			
POLYUNSATURATED FAT	N/A	0.2 G			
CHOLESTEROL	3 MG	2 MG			
FIBER	0 G	0 G			

*Nutritional analyses do not account for substitutions.

**Nutritional analysis does not differ significantly from traditional preparation.

Mozzarella Sticks
with Zesty Pizza Sauce

MAKES 16 MOZZARELLA STICKS

These totally yummy mozzarella sticks can get a little messy if the cheese oozes out of the crumb coating. But they taste so good you won't mind a bit. They're crispy on the outside and packed with flavor—and will rival any restaurant rendition. Serve with Zesty Pizza Sauce (recipe follows) or your favorite marinara sauce. For a more gourmet rendition, smoked mozzarella can be substituted.

3/4 c. egg substitute
   (such as Egg Beaters)
3/4 c. unbleached white flour
1 1/2 c. Italian-seasoned breadcrumbs
Canola cooking spray

1 lb. (454 g) part-skim mozzarella cheese, cut into sticks approximately 3/4 inch wide, 3 inches long, and 1/2 inch thick (to save time, use prepackaged part-skim string cheese)

1. Place the egg substitute, flour, and breadcrumbs in three separate shallow bowls. Preheat the broiler and spray the bottom of a 9- x 13-inch baking pan with canola cooking spray.
2. Dip the mozzarella sticks in the egg substitute, then coat them with flour. Dip back in the egg substitute, then roll in breadcrumbs until very well coated. Lay the mozzarella sticks evenly in the prepared pan as you go. Spray the tops of the cheese sticks with canola cooking spray.
3. Place in the broiler about 4 inches away from the flame and cook until the top side is lightly browned. Flip the cheese sticks, spray with canola cooking spray, and broil for another minute or so until lightly browned. Serve immediately with Zesty Pizza Sauce.

NUTRITIONAL ANALYSES (PER MOZZARELLA STICK)

	BEFORE	AFTER		BEFORE	AFTER
CALORIES	160	127	CHOLESTEROL	15 MG	15 MG
PROTEIN	6 G	11 G	FIBER	0.3 G	0.3 G
CARBOHYDRATES	11 G	9 G	SODIUM	439 MG	280 MG
FAT	10 G	5 G	% CALORIES FROM FAT	56	35
SATURATED FAT	5 G	3.1 G	OMEGA-3 FATTY ACIDS	N/A	0.04 G
MONOUNSATURATED FAT	N/A	1.4 G	OMEGA-6 FATTY ACIDS	N/A	0.1 G
POLYUNSATURATED FAT	N/A	0.14 G			

Zesty Pizza Sauce

MAKES ABOUT 1 1/2 C. (12 SERVINGS, 2 TBSP. PER SERVING)

1 10 3/4-oz. (300 g) can tomato puree
1 tbsp. granulated sugar
2 tsp. olive oil
1/2 tsp. lemon juice
1/4 tsp. salt (optional)

1/2 tsp. dried oregano
1/4 tsp. dried basil
1/4 tsp. dried thyme
2 tsp. minced or chopped garlic

Place all the ingredients in a small, nonstick saucepan and bring to a boil over medium heat. Cover the saucepan, reduce the heat to a simmer, and simmer for 15 minutes. Serve warm.

FRY LIGHT, FRY RIGHT PREPARATION (PER 2 TBSP. SERVING)*

CALORIES	20	FIBER	0.2 G
PROTEIN	0.4 G	SODIUM	6 MG
CARBOHYDRATE	3 G	% CALORIES FROM FAT	36
FAT	0.8 G	OMEGA-3 FATTY ACIDS	0.01 G
SATURATED FAT	0.1 G	OMEGA-6 FATTY ACIDS	0.06 G
MONOUNSATURATED FAT	0.6 G		
POLYUNSATURATED FAT	0.1 G	*Nutritional analysis does not differ significantly	
CHOLESTEROL	0 MG	from traditional preparation.	

Oven-Toasted Ravioli

MAKES ABOUT 42 RAVIOLI

Try this recipe with meat, cheese, or spinach ravioli—all taste terrific! It's important not to overboil the ravioli, but to cook it al dente. This will give them the crispy texture you want when they are baked. Serve with a bottled marinara or pizza sauce, or use Zesty Pizza Sauce (page 53).

Canola cooking spray
1 15-oz. (425 g) package cheese, meat, or
    spinach ravioli (check the label for
    lower fat, if possible)
1 1/2 tbsp. canola oil or olive oil
1 c. plain breadcrumbs
1 tsp. dried parsley

1 1/2 tsp. dried oregano
1/2 tsp. salt, or to taste
1 tsp. garlic powder
1/4 tsp. ground pepper
1/3 c. finely grated Parmesan cheese (if
    shredded, put in food processor for 5
    seconds to process to a coarse powder)

1. Preheat the oven to 400° F (200° C). Coat two 9- x 13-inch baking dishes with canola cooking spray.
2. Drop the ravioli into 2 quarts (9 l) of boiling salted water and boil for 6–8 minutes, or until just tender.
3. Drain the ravioli well and lay in a single layer atop double-thickness paper towels to dry thoroughly. Pat the tops with paper towels or flip the ravioli to dry the other side.
4. Place the ravioli in large bowl. Drizzle with 1 1/2 tablespoons of oil and toss gently to coat well.
5. Place the breadcrumbs, parsley, oregano, salt, garlic powder, pepper, and Parmesan cheese in a medium bowl and stir to blend. Sprinkle the breadcrumb mixture over the ravioli and toss gently to coat the ravioli well.
6. Spread the ravioli in the prepared baking dishes in a single layer. Bake, uncovered, for about 15–20 minutes or until the ravioli are lightly brown and crispy. Cool slightly and serve with warm marinara sauce for dipping.

NUTRITIONAL ANALYSES (PER SERVING; ANALYZED WITH 6 CHEESE RAVIOLI)

	BEFORE	AFTER		BEFORE	AFTER
CALORIES	280	200	CHOLESTEROL	23 MG	22 MG
PROTEIN	9 G	9 G	FIBER	2 G	2 G
CARBOHYDRATES	24 G	24 G	SODIUM	306 MG	306 MG
FAT	16.6 G	7.5 G FAT	% CALORIES FROM FAT	53	34
SATURATED FAT	3.6 G	2.5 G	OMEGA-3 FATTY ACIDS	0.4 G	0.3 G
MONOUNSATURATED FAT	6 G	2.8 G	OMEGA-6 FATTY ACIDS	5.8 G	0.5 G
POLYUNSATURATED FAT	6.3 G	1 G			

Oven-Fried Camembert
with **Raspberry Sauce**

MAKES 6 SERVINGS (2 WEDGES PER SERVING)

This is a beautiful, not to mention delicious, appetizer. And with the golden sesame-crumb coating and the deep red berry topping, it's also quite impressive.

1 8-oz. (230 g) circle Camembert
  or Brie cheese, chilled
1 egg
1/4 c. egg substitute
  (such as Egg Beaters)
2 tbsp. Wondra quick-mixing flour
3/4 c. fine plain breadcrumbs

1/3 c. sesame seeds
  (1 2.6-oz., or 75 g, bottle)
12 foil cupcake papers
Canola cooking spray
1/4 c. raspberry or boysenberry preserves
  (seedless, if possible) or low-sugar jam,
  warmed

1. Preheat the oven to 500° F (260° C). Cut the chilled cheese into 12 equal wedges.
2. In a shallow bowl, whisk together the egg, egg substitute, and Wondra flour until smooth. In another shallow bowl, toss together the breadcrumbs and sesame seeds.
3. Dip each cheese wedge into the egg mixture and turn to coat well. Transfer to the crumb mixture and coat well. Repeat. Set the wedge upright (rind-side down) in foil cupcake paper. Repeat with the remaining cheese wedges.
4. Coat the top and sides of each wedge lightly with canola cooking spray. Bake for about 8 minutes or until the crumb coating is just golden.
5. Let cool for a few minutes. Serve in foil cups or remove to a platter, if desired, dabbing the top of each wedge with a teaspoon of warmed raspberry or boysenberry preserves.

NUTRITIONAL ANALYSES

	BEFORE	AFTER		BEFORE	AFTER
CALORIES	255	205	CHOLESTEROL	70 MG	45 MG
PROTEIN	11.5 G	11 G	FIBER	1 G	1 G
CARBOHYDRATES	14 G	14 G	SODIUM	389 MG	387 MG
FAT	16.5 G	11 G	% CALORIES FROM FAT	58	48
SATURATED FAT	7 G	6 G	OMEGA-3 FATTY ACIDS	0.2 G	0.12 G
MONOUNSATURATED FAT	4.9 G	3.5 G	OMEGA-6 FATTY ACIDS	3.7 G	1 G
POLYUNSATURATED FAT	3.9 G	1.1 G			

Mini Crab Cakes
with Quick Jalapeño-Lime Mayonnaise

MAKES 8 MINI CRAB CAKES

Why take a naturally low-fat food like crab and submerge it in a deep-fat fryer when you can brown it just as nicely in a little bit of canola oil in a frying pan? These appetizers are particularly yummy with fresh crabmeat. The recipe can easily be doubled or tripled.

1 c. plain dried breadcrumbs, divided
1 tbsp. light mayonnaise
1 tbsp. fat-free sour cream
2 tbsp. egg substitute
   (such as Egg Beaters)
2 tsp. Dijon mustard

2 green onions, white and green parts,
   finely chopped
1/2 tsp. Worcestershire sauce
1/2 tsp. Old Bay Seasoning
2 c. fresh crabmeat, picked over for
   cartilage (about 10 oz., or 280 g)
2 tsp. canola oil

1. Place 1/4 c. of the breadcrumbs, along with the mayonnaise, sour cream, egg substitute, mustard, green onions, Worcestershire sauce, and Old Bay Seasoning, in a large bowl. With wet hands, mix in the crabmeat and shape into eight small crab cakes about 1/2 inch thick.
2. Place the remaining breadcrumbs in a shallow bowl. Dip the crab cakes into the bread-crumbs and coat lightly on all sides.
3. In a nonstick medium-sized frying pan over medium-high heat, place 2 teaspoons of canola oil and tilt the pan to cover the bottom evenly. Add the crab cakes and fry until the bottoms are golden brown, about 3 minutes. Flip and brown the other side, about 3 minutes more.
4. Serve with Quick Jalapeño-Lime Mayonnaise (opposite) or the dipping sauce of your choice.

NUTRITIONAL ANALYSES (PER CRAB CAKE)

	BEFORE	AFTER		BEFORE	AFTER
CALORIES	323	188	CHOLESTEROL	113 MG	60 MG
PROTEIN	16.7 G	16 G	FIBER	1 G	1 G
CARBOHYDRATES	16 G	16 G	SODIUM	445 MG	440 MG
FAT	21 G	6 G	% CALORIES FROM FAT	59	28
SATURATED FAT	2.6 G	0.5 G	OMEGA-3 FATTY ACIDS	0.6 G	0.5 G
MONOUNSATURATED FAT	5.4 G	1.6 G	OMEGA-6 FATTY ACIDS	8.6 G	0.5 G
POLYUNSATURATED FAT	9.4 G	1.2 G			

Quick Jalapeño-Lime Mayonnaise

MAKES ABOUT 3/4 C.

2 tbsp. light mayonnaise
1/2 c. fat-free sour cream (Naturally
    Yours brand is best)
2 tbsp. lime juice

1/2 tsp. seeded and minced jalapeño
    pepper, or to taste
1/2 tsp. Dijon mustard
Salt and pepper, to taste

Combine the mayonnaise, sour cream, lime juice, jalapeño, and mustard in a food processor or 2-cup measure. Blend until smooth. Season with salt and pepper to taste and serve, or refrigerate for several days until needed.

NUTRITIONAL ANALYSES (PER SERVING, ABOUT 2 TBSP.)

	BEFORE	AFTER		BEFORE	AFTER
CALORIES	170	38	CHOLESTEROL	12 MG	4 MG
PROTEIN	0.4 G	1 G	FIBER	0.1 G	0.1 G
CARBOHYDRATES	0.7 G	4 G	SODIUM	144 MG	65 MG
FAT	18 G	1.8 G	% CALORIES FROM FAT	95	43
SATURATED FAT	3 G	0.4 G	OMEGA-3 FATTY ACIDS	0.4 G	0.2 G
MONOUNSATURATED FAT	5 G	0.5 G	OMEGA-6 FATTY ACIDS	9.5 G	0.7 G
POLYUNSATURATED FAT	10 G	0.9 G			

Salmon Croquettes with Fresh Dill

MAKES 14 CROQUETTES

We are keeping these croquettes light by shaping them into patties instead of the traditional cylinder shape. This lets us easily pan-fry them in a little bit of canola oil instead of deep-frying them in a vat of hot fat.

1 lb. (454 g) salmon, cooked and flaked (about 1 3/4 c. flaked), or 1 14 3/4-oz. (405 g) can salmon, drained and flaked
1/4 c. minced onion
1 lb. (454 g; about 2 average) Idaho potatoes, peeled, cooked, and mashed (about 1 3/4 c. mashed potatoes)
1 large egg
1/4 c. egg substitute (such as Egg Beaters)
1/4–1/2 tsp. Tabasco sauce, to taste

1/4 tsp. salt (optional)
3 tbsp. chopped fresh dill
1/4 c. cornmeal
1/4 tsp. salt
1/4 tsp. ground black pepper
1 tbsp. canola oil
Canola cooking spray
Lemon wedges
Fast & Light Tartar Sauce (page 122), for serving (optional)

1. In a large bowl, combine the salmon, onion, mashed potatoes, egg, egg substitute, Tabasco, salt (if desired), and fresh dill, and mix well with a fork. Refrigerate for 1–2 hours. (If you're pressed for time, you can proceed directly to step #2 without chilling the mixture; it just won't hold together quite as well.)
2. In a shallow bowl, stir together the cornmeal, salt, and pepper. Use a cookie scoop (1/8 cup) to form a portion of the salmon mixture into a ball. Place the ball in the cornmeal mixture and turn to coat well.
3. Place the canola oil in a large, nonstick skillet and swirl to coat the bottom. Begin to heat the oil over medium-high heat. Add the coated salmon balls to the pan and use the back of a spatula to flatten them into 1/2-inch-thick patties. Spray the tops with canola cooking spray.
4. Cook the patties about 3 minutes per side or until they're crisp and nicely brown. Remove from the heat and serve hot with lemon wedges and Fast & Light Tartar Sauce, if desired.

NUTRITIONAL ANALYSES (PER 2 CROQUETTES)

	BEFORE	AFTER		BEFORE	AFTER
CALORIES	312	183	CHOLESTEROL	95 MG	65 MG
PROTEIN	16.5 G	16 G	FIBER	2 G	2 G
CARBOHYDRATES	14 G	14 G	SODIUM	300 MG	297 MG
FAT	21 G	7 G	% CALORIES FROM FAT	61	34
SATURATED FAT	3.2 G	1.2 G	OMEGA-3 FATTY ACIDS	1.4 G	1.3 G
MONOUNSATURATED FAT	6.5 G	2.9 G	OMEGA-6 FATTY ACIDS	8.8 G	0.8 G
POLYUNSATURATED FAT	10.4 G	2.3 G			

Gingery Shrimp & Vegetable Dumplings

MAKES ABOUT 16 DUMPLINGS

These fragrant dumplings are also great steamed—just skip step #4.

About 5 oz. (140 g) raw shrimp, peeled, deveined, and tails removed
2 tbsp. finely minced carrot
2 tbsp. finely minced green onions
1/2 tsp. minced fresh ginger
1/2 tsp. minced or chopped fresh garlic
1/8 tsp. salt

1/4 tsp. sugar
16 wonton wrappers, (or 4 eggroll wrappers), quartered
1/4 c. egg substitute (such as Egg Beaters) or 1 egg, beaten*
1 tsp. canola oil or canola cooking spray
Soy sauce and rice wine vinegar, for serving (optional)

1. In the bowl of a food processor, place the shrimp, carrot, green onions, ginger, garlic, salt, and sugar. Pulse to blend into a paste-like mixture, pausing a few times to scrape down the sides of the bowl.
2. Measure 1/2 tablespoon of the shrimp mixture into the center of a wonton wrapper. Brush egg substitute around all four edges of the wrapper. Bring up two opposite corners to meet in the middle; bring up the other two corners and press all four together. Press together the edges of the wrapper to seal fairly well, then twist the top gently to make a little dumpling. Repeat with remaining filling and wrappers.
3. Place about 1–1 1/2 inches of water in a large saucepan over high heat. Coat the inside of a metal steamer with canola cooking spray and set into the saucepan (make sure the water does not seep into the basket of the steamer). Once the water boils, place the dumpling onto the metal steamer, cover the saucepan, and cook for about 15 minutes. Test one of the dumplings to make sure the shrimp is completely cooked.
4. Once the shrimp is cooked through, immediately remove the dumplings from the steamer. Coat a medium nonstick frying pan with 1 teaspoon canola oil and place over medium heat. Add the dumplings and brown briefly, about 2–3 minutes.

NUTRITIONAL ANALYSES (PER 4 DUMPLINGS)

	BEFORE	AFTER		BEFORE	AFTER
CALORIES	226	136	CHOLESTEROL	56 MG	56 MG
PROTEIN	11 G	11 G	FIBER	0.2 G	0.2 G
CARBOHYDRATES	20 G	20 G	SODIUM	308 MG	308 MG
FAT	10 G	1 G	% CALORIES FROM FAT	40	8
SATURATED FAT	1.7 G	0.2 G	OMEGA-3 FATTY ACIDS	0.3 G	0.3 G
MONOUNSATURATED FAT	4.4 G	0.2 G	OMEGA-6 FATTY ACIDS	2.9 G	0.1 G
POLYUNSATURATED FAT	3.2 G	0.4 G	*Nutritional analyses do not account for substitutions.		

Baked Butterflied Shrimp
with Tequila Cocktail Sauce
MAKES 6 SERVINGS (ABOUT 4 SHRIMP PER SERVING)

I love shrimp! For this recipe, we are single-coating the shrimp (instead of double-coating, as the original recipe requested) and baking them until crisp. These are delicious with Tequila Cocktail Sauce (recipe follows), but would also be good with a bottled dipping sauce or cocktail sauce of your choice.

2 tbsp. canola oil
3 c. water
1 1/2 c. cornstarch
1 large egg
1/4 c. egg substitute
   (such as Egg Beaters)

2 c. Italian-style breadcrumbs
1/4 c. cornmeal
1 lb. (454 g; about 24) large shrimp,
   peeled, deveined, and butterflied
Canola cooking spray
Tequila Cocktail Sauce (recipe follows)

1. Preheat the oven to 450° F (230° C). Use a pastry brush to coat a 10- x 15-inch nonstick jelly roll pan with canola oil.
2. Place the water in a large bowl and whisk in the cornstarch, egg, and egg substitute until blended well. Place the breadcrumbs and cornmeal in a separate medium-sized bowl.
3. Dip the shrimp into the cornstarch mixture to coat completely. Then roll the shrimp in the breadcrumbs and place on the prepared pan, making sure they don't touch.
4. Coat the top of shrimp well with canola cooking spray. Bake until golden brown and cooked through, about 20 minutes. Serve immediately with Tequila Cocktail Sauce.

NUTRITIONAL ANALYSES (PER SERVING)

	BEFORE	AFTER		BEFORE	AFTER
CALORIES	394	274	CHOLESTEROL	132 MG	132 MG
PROTEIN	19 G	19 G	FIBER	1 G	1 G
CARBOHYDRATES	31 G	31 G	SODIUM	415 MG	415 MG
FAT	20.6 G	7 G	% CALORIES FROM FAT	47	23
SATURATED FAT	2.4 G	0.7 G	OMEGA-3 FATTY ACIDS	0.9 G	0.8 G
MONOUNSATURATED FAT	6.4 G	3.1 G	OMEGA-6 FATTY ACIDS	9 G	1.1 G
POLYUNSATURATED FAT	10 G	2 G			

Tequila Cocktail Sauce

MAKES 2 1/4 C. (18 SERVINGS)

This spicy cocktail sauce with attitude takes just minutes to whip up.

3/4 c. ketchup
3/4 c. bottled chili sauce
1/4 c. bottled horseradish
1/8 c. Worcestershire sauce
3 tbsp. grated onion

1 1/2 tbsp. lemon juice
1 1/2 tsp. Tabasco sauce
1/4 c. tequila
Salt and pepper, to taste

In a medium-sized bowl, stir together the ketchup, chili sauce, horseradish, Worcestershire sauce, onion, lemon juice, Tabasco, and tequila until blended well. Season with salt and pepper to taste and serve, or refrigerate for up to 3 days until needed.

FRY LIGHT, FRY RIGHT PREPARATION (PER TBSP)*

CALORIES	35	SODIUM	460 MG
PROTEIN	0.2 G	% CALORIES FROM FAT	0
CARBOHYDRATE	7 G	OMEGA-3 FATTY ACIDS	0 G
FAT	0 G	OMEGA-6 FATTY ACIDS	0 G
SATURATED FAT	N/A		
MONOUNSATURATED FAT	N/A	*Nutritional analysis does not differ significantly	
POLYUNSATURATED FAT	N/A	from traditional preparation.	
CHOLESTEROL	0 MG		
FIBER	0.3 G		

New England Clam Fritters

MAKES 4 SERVINGS (2 PATTIES PER SERVING)

This fritter recipe does well with either canned or fresh clams. I've lightened these up in a couple of ways. The batter is lower in fat because it uses fat-free half-and-half and egg substitute, and the fritters are pan-fried in just a tablespoon of canola oil.

1 large egg (or 1/4 c. egg substitute such as Egg Beaters)
1/2 c. all-purpose flour
1/3 c. fat-free half-and-half or low-fat milk
1 c. cooked minced clams, drained (3 cans, each 6.5 oz. or 185 g)
1/4 tsp. salt

1/8 tsp. ground black pepper
1/4 c. finely chopped onion
1/4 c. finely minced red bell pepper
1 tbsp. canola oil
Canola cooking spray

1. In a medium bowl, beat the egg and gradually beat in the flour. Slowly stir in the half-and-half, clams, salt, pepper, onion, and red bell pepper.
2. Place the canola oil in a large nonstick skillet over medium-high heat and tilt the pan to coat the bottom evenly with oil. When the oil is hot, use a cookie scoop (1/8 cup) to drop the batter into the hot pan (the fritters will be around 3 inches wide). Pan-fry the fritters until the bottoms are golden brown, about 4 minutes. Coat the tops lightly with canola cooking spray and flip the fritters over with a spatula. Brown the other side (about 3 minutes more), remove from the heat, and serve.

NUTRITIONAL ANALYSES (PER SERVING)

	BEFORE	AFTER		BEFORE	AFTER
CALORIES	236	146	CHOLESTEROL	63 MG	63 MG
PROTEIN	9 G	9 G	FIBER	1 G	1 G
CARBOHYDRATES	16.5 G	16.5 G	SODIUM	470 MG	470 MG
FAT	15 G	4.8 G	% CALORIES FROM FAT	57	29
SATURATED FAT	2 G	0.7 G	OMEGA-3 FATTY ACIDS	0.4 G	0.3 G
MONOUNSATURATED FAT	3 G	2.6 G	OMEGA-6 FATTY ACIDS	6.8 G	0.9 G
POLYUNSATURATED FAT	7.2 G	1.2 G			

Spicy Pan-Fried Oysters

MAKES 10 OYSTERS

I've always been a little spooked at the idea of handling raw oysters, but once I got past it and battered and pan-fried them, I was delighted! These are really delicious. Because we use a batter and not a crumb coating, we have to pan-fry them in a wee bit of canola oil instead of baking them in the oven.

1 c. (about 10 oysters) shucked
    raw oysters, with 1/4 c. oyster juice
    reserved
2 tbsp. egg substitute
    (such as Egg Beaters)
1/2 tsp. ground black pepper

1/2 tsp. Old Bay Seasoning
    (or similar spice blend)
6 tbsp. Reduced Fat Bisquick pancake mix
1 tbsp. canola oil
Lemon wedges and finely chopped fresh
    parsley, for serving

1. In a medium-sized bowl, combine the oysters, reserved oyster juice, egg substitute, pepper, and Old Bay Seasoning. Gently stir in the pancake mix to make a nice batter.
2. Place the canola oil in a medium, nonstick frying pan over medium-high heat.
3. When the oil is hot, use a slotted spoon to place the oysters, one at a time, into the pan. Make sure there is enough batter surrounding each oyster to coat it nicely. Fry the oysters until golden brown on the bottom, about 3 minutes, then flip and brown the other side— about 3 minutes more.
4. Remove from the heat and serve immediately with lemon wedges and a sprinkle of fresh finely chopped parsley, if desired.

NUTRITIONAL ANALYSES (PER 2 OYSTERS)

	BEFORE	AFTER		BEFORE	AFTER
CALORIES	155	95	CHOLESTEROL	68 MG	26 MG
PROTEIN	5.5 G	5 G	FIBER	0.1 G	0.1 G
CARBOHYDRATES	8 G	8 G	SODIUM	223 MG	221 MG
FAT	11 G	4.5 G	% CALORIES FROM FAT	64	42
SATURATED FAT	1.8	0.7 G	OMEGA-3 FATTY ACIDS	0.7 G	0.6 G
MONOUNSATURATED FAT	3.5 G	1.8 G	OMEGA-6 FATTY ACIDS	3.8 G	0.6 G
POLYUNSATURATED FAT	4.6 G	1.3 G			

Better-for-You Buffalo Chicken Wings with Light Blue Cheese Dip

MAKES 7 SERVINGS (4 WING DRUMETTES PER SERVING)

Everyone seems to love Buffalo wings, and this recipe is a big hit whenever I serve it! Fast-food versions contain around 315 calories and 22 grams of fat for four wings, largely because they're deep-fried with the skin on. To make this more healthful version, we have removed the skin and decreased the cooking oil, instead coating the wings with a touch of canola cooking spray.

2 tsp. seasoned salt (Lawry's brand is good)
2 tsp. chili powder
2 tsp. garlic powder
1 tsp. freshly ground pepper
2 tbsp. flour
2 1/2 lb. (1100 g, or about 28) wing drumettes

Canola cooking spray
1/4 c. nonalcoholic beer or light beer (chicken broth or wine can also be used)
Light Blue Cheese Dip (recipe follows) or light ranch dressing, for serving (optional)

1. In a small mixing bowl, stir together the seasoned salt, chili powder, garlic powder, pepper, and flour. Remove and discard the skin from the wings. Dip each wing into the seasoning mixture, pressing the mixture onto the chicken to coat well.
2. Generously coat a large nonstick skillet with canola cooking spray and place over medium-high heat. Add the chicken wings (cooking in batches if necessary) and cook for about 4 minutes, or until the bottoms are browned. Flip with prongs and cook for about 4 minutes more.
3. Reduce the heat to medium-low and add the beer. Cover the pan and cook for about 5 minutes. If the wings aren't cooked through, turn them over and cook for a few minutes more. Remove from the heat and serve hot with Light Blue Cheese Dip or light ranch dressing, if desired.

NUTRITIONAL ANALYSES (PER 4 WING DRUMETTES)

	BEFORE	AFTER		BEFORE	AFTER
CALORIES	197	174	CHOLESTEROL	52 MG	73 MG
PROTEIN	17 G	29 G	FIBER	0 G	0 G
CARBOHYDRATES	2 G	2 G	SODIUM	551 MG	539 MG
FAT	14 G	4.5 G	% CALORIES FROM FAT	64	23
SATURATED FAT	3.6 G	1.2 G	OMEGA-3 FATTY ACIDS	0.3 G	0.1
MONOUNSATURATED FAT	5.3 G	1.1 G	OMEGA-6 FATTY ACIDS	3.2 G	0.8 G
POLYUNSATURATED FAT	3.5 G	1 G			

Light Blue Cheese Dip

MAKES ABOUT 3/4 C. (6 SERVINGS)

2 tbsp. blue cheese (plus an extra tbsp., if desired)

1/4 c. low-fat or light mayonnaise

6 tbsp. low-fat buttermilk

1/4 c. fat-free sour cream

1/8 tsp. ground black pepper, or to taste

1/8 tsp. onion powder

1/8 tsp. garlic powder

In a small bowl, mix all the ingredients together by hand. If a creamier dip is desired, place the ingredients in the bowl of a food processor and pulse until smooth. Cover the bowl and refrigerate for several days until needed.

NUTRITIONAL ANALYSES (PER 2 TBSP.)

	BEFORE	AFTER		BEFORE	AFTER
CALORIES	154	42	CHOLESTEROL	5 MG	4 MG
PROTEIN	1.5 G	2 G	FIBER	0 G	0 G
CARBOHYDRATES	2.3 G	5 G	SODIUM	335 MG	156 MG
FAT	16 G	1.7 G	% CALORIES FROM FAT	93	36
SATURATED FAT	3 G	0.7 G	OMEGA-3 FATTY ACIDS	1.1 G	0.01 G
MONOUNSATURATED FAT	3.8 G	0.3 G	OMEGA-6 FATTY ACIDS	7.2 G	0.02 G
POLYUNSATURATED FAT	8.5 G	0.03 G			

Turkey Pot Stickers with Super Easy Sweet & Sour Sauce

MAKES ABOUT 4 SERVINGS (5 POT STICKERS PER SERVING)

One of the things I love about pot stickers is their crispy browned bottoms. With these fragrantly seasoned pot stickers, we keep this crispy bottom, but cut the fat. Instead of frying these through, we are going to pan-fry them briefly in a minimal amount of canola oil, then add some water and finish the cooking process by steaming.

1/4 lb. (110 g) ground lean or
    extra-lean turkey
1/2 tsp. fresh minced ginger
2 tbsp. minced green onions
2 tbsp. finely minced water chestnuts
1 tsp. lower-sodium soy sauce
1/2 tsp. ground black pepper
1/4 tsp. crushed red pepper flakes (can
    remove seeds for less heat)

1/4 tsp. salt (optional)
1 tsp. minced garlic
1/4 c. egg substitute
    (such as Egg Beaters), divided
20 round wonton wrappers
    (Azumaya brand is good)
    for pot stickers and dumplings
2 tsp. canola oil
2 c. hot water

1. In a medium bowl, combine the ground turkey, ginger, green onions, water chestnuts, soy sauce, black pepper, red pepper flakes, salt (if desired), and garlic; mix well. Stir in 1 tablespoon of the egg substitute; pour the remaining egg substitute into a small cup or bowl.
2. Stack the wrappers on a clean work area and cover with a damp cloth. Lay one wrapper on a flat surface and spoon a slightly heaping teaspoon of filling just off-center.
3. Wet the edges of the wrap with the remaining egg substitute. Fold the wrapper over the filling and seal the edges with a crimp-and-seal tool or with the tines of a fork. Give the pot sticker a flat bottom by holding the seam straight up and gently pressing the bottom of the pot sticker into a flat surface.

NUTRITIONAL ANALYSES (PER SERVING)

	BEFORE	AFTER		BEFORE	AFTER
CALORIES	244	164	CHOLESTEROL	25 MG	25 MG
PROTEIN	9 G	9 G	FIBER	1 G	1 G
CARBOHYDRATES	19.5 G	19.5 G	SODIUM	276 MG	276 MG
FAT	14.1 G	5 G	% CALORIES FROM FAT	52	27
SATURATED FAT	2 G	0.9 G	OMEGA-3 FATTY ACIDS	0.3 G	0.3 G
MONOUNSATURATED FAT	4.5 G	2.3 G	OMEGA-6 FATTY ACIDS	6.5 G	1.2 G
POLYUNSATURATED FAT	6.8 G	1.5 G			

4. Repeat with the remaining filling and wraps.
5. Coat a large nonstick frying pan or skillet with the canola oil and place over medium-high heat. When the oil is hot, add the pot stickers to the pan, seams pointing up. Let them sizzle and the bottoms brown for a minute or two. Add the hot water, cover the pan, and continue to cook until the pot stickers are al dente and crisp on bottom and the water is almost evaporated, about 8 minutes.
6. Remove from the heat and serve immediately with Super-Easy Sweet & Sour Sauce or any of the other dipping sauces (such as Orange Hoisin Sauce, page 44, or Mango Ginger Sauce, page 45) in this book.

Super Easy Sweet & Sour Sauce

MAKES 1 C.

Two ingredients and a few minutes are all it takes to make tasty sweet-and-sour sauce. I personally love to dip my egg rolls and pot stickers in this sauce, so let's just say I make it a lot!

1/2 c. chili sauce (Heinz brand is good)
1/2 c. red currant jelly

In a small, nonstick saucepan, stir together the chili sauce and currant jelly. Place the pan over medium heat and bring the mixture to an almost-boil. Reduce to a simmer, cover the pan, and let cook, stirring occasionally, for about 3 minutes more. Let the sauce cool and serve or refrigerate for several days until needed.

FRY LIGHT, FRY RIGHT PREPARATION (PER TBSP.)*

CALORIES	35	FIBER	0 G
PROTEIN	0 G	SODIUM	240 MG
CARBOHYDRATE	9 G	% CALORIES FROM FAT	0
FAT	0 G	OMEGA-3 FATTY ACIDS	0 G
SATURATED FAT	N/A	OMEGA-6 FATTY ACIDS	0 G
MONOUNSATURATED FAT	N/A		
POLYUNSATURATED FAT	N/A	*Nutritional analysis does not differ significantly	
CHOLESTEROL	0 MG	from traditional preparation.	

Crispy Roast Chicken & Pork Lumpia

MAKES 15 SERVINGS (ABOUT 2 LUMPIA PER SERVING)

Lumpia are egg rolls from the Philippines, and this is a lightened version of a family recipe handed down to a Filipino friend by her grandmother. Spring roll wrappers are the best to use, since they are thinner and lighter than egg roll wrappers (in a pinch, however, egg roll wrappers work just fine). You can make a batch of these, bake them, and freeze some for later. They can be reheated for a few minutes in the microwave or toaster oven for a quick snack, appetizer, or side dish (though if using the microwave, the lumpia won't be as crisp). These are wonderful served with a dipping sauce like Super-Easy Sweet & Sour Sauce (page 67), or another sauce of your choosing.

4 tbsp. canola oil, divided

1 lb. (454 g) pork tenderloin, cut into
    1/2-inch cubes

3 c. finely diced roasted, skinless chicken
    breast (if necessary, use some thigh
    meat to bring the total up to 3 c.)

1/2 head cabbage, shredded (about 4 c.)

4 carrots, peeled and diced (about 2 c.)

1/2 tsp. salt, or to taste

1/2 tsp. ground black pepper, or to taste

30 spring roll wrappers (large square
    egg roll wrappers can be substituted)

2 tbsp. unbleached white flour

2 tbsp. water

1. Preheat the oven to 450° F (230° C). Use a pastry brush to coat the bottom of a 10- x 15-inch jelly roll pan with 2 tablespoons of the canola oil.

2. In a large nonstick skillet over medium-high heat, sauté the pork in the remaining 2 teaspoons of canola oil until evenly brown, about 7 minutes. Stir in the diced chicken, shredded cabbage, and diced carrots. Cook over medium heat until the cabbage is tender, about 5 minutes. Remove from the heat, add salt and pepper to taste, and allow to cool slightly while you separate the wrappers.

3. Stack the wrappers on a clean work area and cover with a damp cloth. In a small bowl, combine the flour and water to make a paste. Lay one wrapper on a flat surface with one corner facing you, and spoon about 1/4 cup filling about 2 inches from the bottom corner. Shape the filling horizontally into a long sausage shape. Fold the bottom corner over the

filling and roll upward one turn so the filling is completely encased. Moisten the left and right corners of the triangle with the flour paste, fold in the corners, and press down firmly to seal, creating an envelope. Moisten the top corner of the skin with the flour paste and give one more turn, sealing the cylinder.

4. One by one, place the lumpia in the prepared pan and roll them around in the oil to lightly coat the exterior; remove to a separate plate until all are coated. When ready, return the lumpia to the pan, making sure they do not touch each other. Bake until golden brown, about 20 minutes. (If you decide to bake these in two batches, you don't need to add more oil to the pan—there should still be enough left.) Remove from the oven and serve hot.

NUTRITIONAL ANALYSES (PER SERVING)

	BEFORE	AFTER		BEFORE	AFTER
CALORIES	254	174	CHOLESTEROL	26 MG	26 MG
PROTEIN	13 G	13 G	FIBER	2 G	2 G
CARBOHYDRATES	21 G	21 G	SODIUM	289 MG	289 MG
FAT	13.1 G	4 G	% CALORIES FROM FAT	46	21
SATURATED FAT	1.8 G	0.6 G	OMEGA-3 FATTY ACIDS	0.3 G	0.3 G
MONOUNSATURATED FAT	4.1 G	1.9 G	OMEGA-6 FATTY ACIDS	6.2 G	0.9 G
POLYUNSATURATED FAT	6.5 G	1.2 G			

Roast Chicken, Pepper
& Onion Empanadas

MAKES 16 EMPANADAS

Empanada is Spanish for "to bake in pastry." These tiny meat pies traditionally contain onion and peppers, but the fillings—such as beef, chicken, and fish—vary, as do the spices. Empanadas with fish filling are especially popular in Spain, but for our version I've used something a bit more kid-friendly: roast chicken. This version has just a touch of spice and an easy-to-work-with pie dough, which makes it adult-friendly, too. You can buy a roast chicken from a local rotisserie or supermarket deli if you're pressed for time.

Canola cooking spray
2 tsp. olive oil (optional)
2 roast chicken breasts, skinned and
    boned, meat finely diced
1/2 c. finely chopped green, red, or yellow
    bell pepper
1/2 c. finely chopped onion
1 tsp. chopped or pressed garlic

1 c. chopped seeded, diced tomatoes
1/2 tsp. paprika (optional)
1/2 tsp. salt (optional)
Freshly ground pepper (optional)
2 prepared piecrusts (refrigerated folded
    crusts such as the 15-oz., or 425 g,
    Pillsbury brand work well)

1. Preheat the oven to 375° F (190° C). Coat a cookie sheet with canola cooking spray. Coat a large nonstick skillet with canola cooking spray or 2 teaspoons olive oil. Add the chicken, bell pepper, onion, and garlic, and cook until the onion is tender, about 4 minutes (add a tablespoon or two of water if moisture is needed). Stir in the tomatoes, paprika, salt, and pepper and cook for another minute or two. Set aside to cool.
2. Unfold the piecrusts and use a 4-inch circular cutter to cut the dough into 4-inch rounds. Gather any scraps of dough and roll out; cut as many 4-inch circles as possible.
3. Place 1/8 cup of the meat filling on half a circle of dough. Fold over the other half and seal the edges with the tines of a fork. Place the meat-filled pastry on the prepared baking sheet. Repeat until all the dough circles have been filled.

4. Place the cookie sheet into the preheated oven and bake the empanadas until both the tops and bottoms are lightly browned, about 20 minutes. Remove from the oven and serve hot or at room temperature.

NUTRITIONAL ANALYSES (PER EMPANADA)

	BEFORE	AFTER		BEFORE	AFTER
CALORIES	176	136	CHOLESTEROL	9 MG	9 MG
PROTEIN	5 G	5 G	FIBER	1 G	1 G
CARBOHYDRATES	13 G	13 G	SODIUM	173 MG	173 MG
FAT	11.5 G	7 G	% CALORIES FROM FAT	59	46
SATURATED FAT	2.6 G	2 G	OMEGA-3 FATTY ACIDS	0.3 G	0.3 G
MONOUNSATURATED FAT	5.1 G	4 G	OMEGA-6 FATTY ACIDS	3.2 G	0.6 G
POLYUNSATURATED FAT	3.7 G	1 G			

Seven-Spice Beef Samosas

MAKES 22 SERVINGS (1 SAMOSA PER SERVING)

When I spotted the original recipe for these samosas, I noticed that the chef claimed no better samosas were to be found in the shops of India. That certainly piqued my curiosity. In our healthier version, we're using lean beef to keep the filling nice and light, then wrapping it in a naturally low-fat phyllo dough, lightly coating the outside with canola oil, and baking until crisp. Plan ahead if you're using frozen dough, which must thaw for five hours at room temperature or overnight in the refrigerator. And please don't be intimidated by the ingredients list—these are pretty quick to put together, and the result is savory and satisfying.

4 c. cubed peeled potatoes (about 2 large potatoes)

1 c. peas, fresh or frozen

1 c. finely chopped onions

1 lb. (454 g) ground sirloin or superlean beef

4 tsp. minced or chopped garlic

1 tbsp. minced fresh gingerroot (1 tsp. ground)

1/2 tsp. ground black pepper

1 tsp. salt

1/2 tsp. ground cumin

1/2 tsp. ground coriander

1/2 tsp. ground turmeric

1/2 tsp. chili powder

1/2 tsp. ground cinnamon

1/2 tsp. ground cardamom

2 tbsp. chopped fresh cilantro

2 tbsp. chopped green chili peppers (seeds can be removed for less heat)

1 16-oz. (454 g) package phyllo dough, refrigerated or frozen (see headnote)

1 tbsp. canola oil (optional)

1. Bring a medium saucepan of lightly salted water to a boil. Stir in the potatoes and peas and cook until the potatoes are tender but still firm, about 15 minutes. Drain, mash together, and set aside. (You can also microwave the potatoes and peas on high in a covered dish until the potatoes are tender, about 18 minutes.)
2. Place the onions and ground beef in a large nonstick saucepan over medium-high heat and cook until the beef is evenly brown and the onions are soft, about 5 minutes. Mix in the

garlic, fresh gingerroot, black pepper, salt, cumin, coriander, turmeric, chili powder, cinnamon, and cardamom. Stir in the mashed potato mixture. Remove from the heat and chill in the refrigerator for 1 hour, or until cool.

3. Preheat the oven to 450° F (230° C). Mix the cilantro and green chili peppers into the potato-beef mixture.

4. Remove the phyllo dough from the package and place it under a sheet of waxed paper; cover with a damp towel. Lay a single sheet of phyllo dough out on a clean, flat surface and fold in half widthwise (when folded, the sheet should be almost square). Place approximately 1/4 cup of filling in a lengthwise sausage shape in the center; fold over the short sides and one long side. Roll up to create a 3- to 4-inch-long cylinder, and seal the edges by pressing the dough together with water-moistened fingers.

5. Place the samosas on a nonstick baking sheet that has been well coated with canola cooking spray. Coat the top of the samosas with the spray or lightly brush with some canola oil. Bake for about 20–30 minutes or until golden brown. Serve immediately.

NUTRITIONAL ANALYSES (PER SERVINGS)

	BEFORE	AFTER		BEFORE	AFTER
CALORIES	167	127	CHOLESTEROL	11 MG	11 MG
PROTEIN	7 G	7 G	FIBER	2 G	2 G
CARBOHYDRATES	21 G	21 G	SODIUM	236 MG	236 MG
FAT	6 G	1.5 G	% CALORIES FROM FAT	41	11
SATURATED FAT	1 G	0.4 G	OMEGA-3 FATTY ACIDS	0.1 G	0.1 G
MONOUNSATURATED FAT	1.6 G	0.5 G	OMEGA-6 FATTY ACIDS	2.8 G	0.2 G
POLYUNSATURATED FAT	3.1 G	0.4 G			

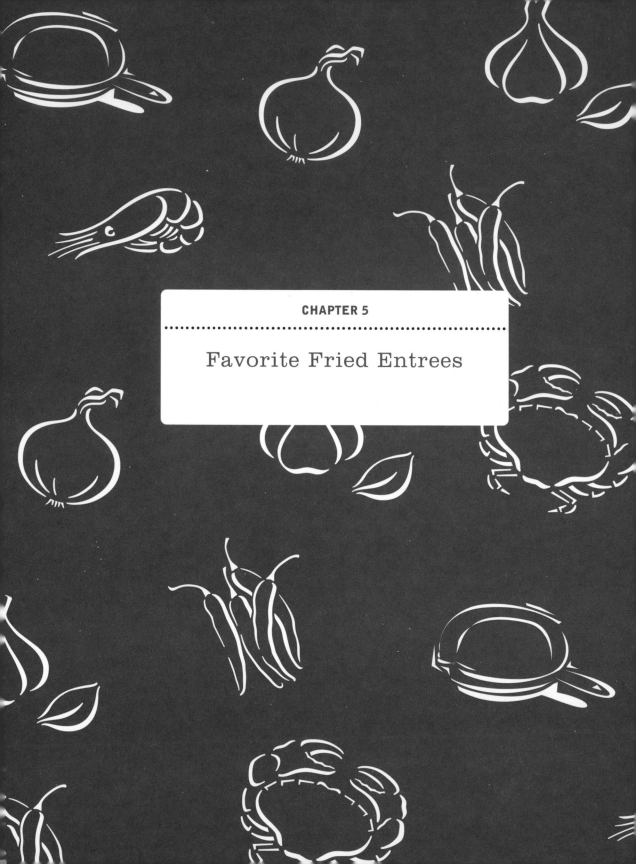

CHAPTER 5

Favorite Fried Entrees

Light Eggplant Parmesan

MAKES 3 SERVINGS

Eggplant Parmesan is one of my favorite nonmeat dishes. It's savory, it's cheesy . . . you won't even miss the meat (at least I don't). I added a layer of roasted red peppers and caramelized onions for a little extra flavor and nutrients. You can double the recipe and freeze half for a hectic weeknight. A serving of traditional eggplant Parmesan contains around 30 grams of fat and 480 calories; this light version contains just 15 grams of fat and 320 calories. There's a big difference in the numbers, but not in the taste.

Canola or olive oil cooking spray
2 small eggplants (about 1 lb., or 454 g)
1/2 c. egg substitute (such as Egg Beaters) or 2 eggs, beaten*
2/3 c. plain breadcrumbs (French or similar); see note
1/2 tsp. seasoning salt
3/4 tsp. garlic powder with parsley (or 1/2 tsp. garlic powder and 1/4 tsp. dried parsley)
1/4 tsp. black pepper

2 tsp. olive oil, divided (flavored olive oils can be substituted)
1/2 large onion, peeled and sliced into rings
1 1/2 c. bottled marinara sauce (lower-sodium marinara can be substituted*)
6 tbsp. shredded Parmesan cheese
1/2 c. roasted red pepper strips (half of a 7.25-oz., or 200 g, jar), drained
1/2 c. packed shredded part-skim mozzarella cheese
Fresh parsley, for garnish (optional)

1. Preheat the oven to 375° F (190° C). Coat a 9-inch loaf pan with cooking spray.
2. Cut the eggplant crosswise into slices about 1/4 inch thick. Place the egg substitute in a shallow bowl. In a second shallow bowl, combine the breadcrumbs, seasoning salt, garlic powder, and black pepper; stir to blend well.
3. Dip each eggplant slice in the egg substitute (covering both sides well), then in the bread-crumb mixture (coating both sides well), and set aside on a plate or waxed paper.
4. Coat the bottom of a large nonstick frying pan with 1 teaspoon of the olive oil and place over medium heat. Evenly distribute half of the eggplant slices in the pan. Coat the tops of the eggplant slices with cooking spray. Cook until the bottoms of the slices are lightly browned, then flip and brown the other side—about 8 minutes per side. When done, remove the slices from the pan and repeat with the remaining olive oil and eggplant slices.

5. Meanwhile, place a small, nonstick frying pan over medium heat. Coat the bottom with cooking spray and add the onion slices. Coat the tops of the onion slices with cooking spray. Cook for about 3 minutes per side, until the onions are soft and lightly brown. Remove the pan from the heat.
6. Add about four eggplant slices to the prepared loaf pan and cover with 1/2 cup of the marinara sauce. Sprinkle with 3 tablespoons of Parmesan. Top with the roasted red pepper strips and browned onion slices. Top with four more eggplant slices, then the remaining marinara sauce, the mozzarella cheese, and the remaining Parmesan.
7. Bake, covered, for 25 minutes or until the cheese and sauce are bubbling. Let rest for 10 minutes. Garnish with fresh parsley and serve.
• NOTE: If you'd prefer to use seasoned breadcrumbs, just omit the seasoning salt, garlic powder, and black pepper.

NUTRITIONAL ANALYSES (PER SERVING)

	BEFORE	AFTER		BEFORE	AFTER
CALORIES	479	323	CHOLESTEROL	82 MG	20 MG
PROTEIN	21 G	17 G	FIBER	5 G	8 G
CARBOHYDRATES	26 G	31 G	SODIUM	1025 MG	1000 MG
FAT	33 G	15 G	% CALORIES FROM FAT	62	41
SATURATED FAT	14 G	5 G	OMEGA-3 FATTY ACIDS	0.6 G	0.6 G
MONOUNSATURATED FAT	12 G	6 G	OMEGA-6 FATTY ACIDS	5.3 G	0.6 G
POLYUNSATURATED FAT	6 G	3.9 G			

*Nutritional analyses do not account for substitutions.

Chiles Rellenos with Garden Salsa

MAKES 5 SERVINGS (ABOUT 2 RELLENOS PER SERVING)

Usually, chiles rellenos are stuffed with regular-fat Monterey Jack cheese and deep-fried. We'll lighten this traditionally oily entrée by using reduced-fat Jack and frying the rellenos until golden brown in a nonstick skillet with only a table-spoon of canola oil. This technique works remarkably well (and provides a good alternative for people who normally have to skip this delicious dish due to medical issues). Serve with Garden Salsa (recipe follows).

14 oz. (400 g) canned fire-roasted whole
    green chilies (Ortega brand is good)
6 oz. (170 g) reduced-fat Monterey Jack
    cheese, cut into 1/4-inch-thick slices
1/2 c. flour
1/4 c. condensed low-sodium chicken broth
1 small onion, peeled and chopped
2 tsp. minced garlic
1 1/2 c. tomato puree

1/2 tsp. dried oregano
Black pepper, to taste
4 large egg whites
1/2 tsp. salt
2 large egg yolks
1/4 c. egg substitute
    (such as Egg Beaters)
About 1 tbsp. canola oil, or more
    as necessary

1. Drain the chilies and place them on paper towels. Insert a slice of cheese into each chili. Roll the chilies generously in flour and set aside.
2. Place a medium saucepan over medium heat and add the broth, onion, and garlic; cook until the garlic and onion are lightly browned, about 3 minutes. Add the tomato puree and oregano, stir, and season with black pepper to taste. Reduce the heat to a simmer, cover the saucepan, and cook for 10 minutes. Remove from the heat and set aside.
3. For the egg coating, whip the egg whites in a mixing bowl with 1/2 teaspoon salt until firm peaks form. In a 2-cup measure, blend the yolks and egg substitute together well. Fold the egg yolk mixture into the whipped egg whites.
4. Place a large nonstick skillet over medium-high heat. Add a tablespoon of canola oil and

NUTRITIONAL ANALYSES (PER SERVING)

	BEFORE	AFTER		BEFORE	AFTER
CALORIES	365	260	CHOLESTEROL	168 MG	109 MG
PROTEIN	17 G	18 G	FIBER	1.3 G	4.5 G
CARBOHYDRATES	8.2 G	21 G	SODIUM	735 MG	735 MG
FAT	30 G	13 G	% CALORIES FROM FAT	74	45
SATURATED FAT	12.5 G	5.8 G	OMEGA-3 FATTY ACIDS	0.5 G	0.4 G
MONOUNSATURATED FAT	9 G	2 G	OMEGA-6 FATTY ACIDS	6.2 G	1.1 G
POLYUNSATURATED FAT	6.7 G	1.5 G			

spread it evenly over the bottom of the skillet. Dip the cheese-filled chilies into the egg coating and place in the pan. Quickly repeat the dipping process until the pan is filled with a layer of chilies. (Use a spoon to spread a bit of egg batter over any chilies that may have lost some their batter.) Coat the tops lightly with canola cooking spray. After about 2 minutes, or when the bottoms are nicely browned, carefully flip the chilies with a spatula. Brown on other side and remove from the heat. Repeat with the remaining chilies (first adding a teaspoon of oil to the pan if necessary).

5. Divide the rellenos among plates and top with a nice spoonful of sauce; or place them in a 9- x 13-inch pan, top with the sauce, and bake in a 350° F oven (175° C) for about 15 minutes. Serve with Garden Salsa.

Garden Salsa

MAKES ABOUT 2 1/2 C.

2 large tomatoes, cored and diced	1 tbsp. white vinegar
1/2 c. chopped mild or sweet onion	1 1/2 tbsp. chopped fresh cilantro
1 tsp. minced or chopped garlic	1/8 tsp. salt
3 tbsp. canned diced green chilies	1/8 tsp. black pepper

In the bowl of a food processor, combine the tomatoes, onion, garlic, chilies, vinegar, cilantro, salt, and pepper, and pulse until blended but still chunky. Place in a bowl and serve, or cover and refrigerate for a few days until needed.

FRY LIGHT, FRY RIGHT PREPARATION (PER 1/4 C.)*

CALORIES	16	FIBER	1 G
PROTEIN	0.7 G	SODIUM	35 MG
CARBOHYDRATE	3.5 G	% CALORIES FROM FAT	8
FAT	0.2 G	OMEGA-3 FATTY ACIDS	0 G
SATURATED FAT	0 G	OMEGA-6 FATTY ACIDS	0.06 G
MONOUNSATURATED FAT	0.02 G		
POLYUNSATURATED FAT	0.06 G	*Nutritional analysis does not differ significantly from
CHOLESTEROL	0 MG	traditional preparation.

Baked Falafels with Tahini Dressing

MAKES ABOUT 5 SERVINGS (5 FALAFEL BALLS PER SERVING)

The main ingredient in falafel is a healthy whole grain called bulgur, which is dried cracked wheat. When I was at graduate school in Berkeley, California, I dabbled in vegetarianism for a few years. During that time, one of the things I enjoyed often was falafel, which was sold in several small restaurants there. The spicy chickpea-bulgur dough is usually dropped by small pieces into deep fat to cook. I added a step—rolling the dough pieces into some crumbs, then oven-baking them at a high temperature. They taste almost exactly the same.

Make a delicious and satisfying pocket sandwich by adding falafels, shredded lettuce, chopped tomato, and some Tahini Dressing (recipe follows) to the inside of a pita. Or serve the falafels as an appetizer with toothpicks and Tahini Dressing as a dip.

1/2 c. fine bulgur wheat (such as Grain Gourmet's Side Dish Solutions, available in many supermarkets)
1 15-oz. (425 g) can garbanzo beans (chickpeas), drained and rinsed (about 1 1/2 c.)
1/2 c. chopped green onions
1/4 c. whole wheat flour
1 large egg

1/4 c. loosely packed chopped parsley
1 1/2 tsp. minced or chopped garlic
1 1/2 tsp. ground cumin
3/4 tsp. red pepper flakes
1/2 tsp. salt
1/2 c. finely ground Italian-style or plain breadcrumbs
Canola cooking spray

1. Place the bulgur in a medium bowl and pour in boiling water to cover it by 2 inches (around 1 1/2 cups). Let soak for about 15 minutes.
2. In the bowl of a food processor, combine the garbanzo beans, green onions, whole wheat flour, egg, parsley, garlic, cumin, red pepper flakes, and salt. Pulse to form a coarse puree.
3. Drain the soaked bulgur (there should now be about 3/4 cup) by removing it from the bowl with a slotted spoon. Add the bulgur to the food processor mixture, 1/4 cup at a time, pulsing after each addition, until the mixture is thick enough to form into balls.

NUTRITIONAL ANALYSES (PER SERVING)

	BEFORE	AFTER		BEFORE	AFTER
CALORIES	300	182	CHOLESTEROL	42 MG	42 MG
PROTEIN	9 G	9 G	FIBER	4 G	6 G
CARBOHYDRATES	31 G	31 G	SODIUM	696 MG	696 MG
FAT	16.4	2.8 G	% CALORIES FROM FAT	49	14
SATURATED FAT	2.1 G	0.4 G	OMEGA-3 FATTY ACIDS	0.1 G	0.02 G
MONOUNSATURATED FAT	3.7 G	0.4 G	OMEGA-6 FATTY ACIDS	8.2 G	0.27 G
POLYUNSATURATED FAT	8.3 G	0.3 G			

4. Place the breadcrumbs in a small bowl. Use a small spoon to scoop a 1-inch ball of falafel dough and drop it into the breadcrumbs; roll it around in the breadcrumbs to lightly coat. Place the coated falafel on a sheet of waxed paper on the counter. Repeat with the remaining falafel dough. Cover the falafels loosely and let them stand for 1 hour.
5. Preheat oven to 450° F (230° C). While still on the waxed paper, coat the tops of the falafels with cooking spray. Play the falafels cooking-spray-side down on a cookie sheet. Spray the tops of the falafels with more cooking spray (they should be almost completely coated, though lightly, with cooking spray).
6. Bake until golden brown, about 20–22 minutes. While they are baking, you can whip up a batch of Tahini Dressing.

Tahini Dressing

MAKES ABOUT 1/2 C.

This dressing tastes really different if you've never had it before, but I promise it will start to grow on you. It goes very well with falafels, either as a dip or as a dressing in a pita bread sandwich.

1/4 c. water
1/4 c. tahini (sesame paste, available in some supermarkets and specialty stores), at room temperature and stirred to smooth

2 tbsp. fresh lemon juice
1/2 tsp. minced or chopped garlic
1/8 tsp. salt
1/4 tsp. Tabasco sauce
2 tsp. honey

Place all the dressing ingredients in a blender, small food processor bowl, or small mixing bowl; beat or pulse until well blended (it should look whipped). Place in a bowl and serve, or cover and refrigerate up to 3 days.

FRY LIGHT, FRY RIGHT PREPARATION (PER TBSP.)*

CALORIES	51	FIBER	0.4 G
PROTEIN	2 G	SODIUM	38 MG
CARBOHYDRATE	3.5 G	% CALORIES FROM FAT	67
FAT	3.8 G	OMEGA-3 FATTY ACIDS	0.03 G
SATURATED FAT	0.6 G	OMEGA-6 FATTY ACIDS	1.7 G
MONOUNSATURATED FAT	1.5 G		
POLYUNSATURATED FAT	1.7 G	*Nutritional analysis does not differ significantly from
CHOLESTEROL	0 MG	traditional preparation.

Fresh Mex Soft Fish Tacos

MAKES 4 SERVINGS (2 TACOS PER SERVING)

Serve these yummy tacos with Salsa Guacamole (page 103) and seasoned pinto beans.

1 1-oz. (30 g) envelope fish taco seasoning or taco seasoning

1 lb. (454 g) skinless, boneless white fish such as halibut, cod, sole, or orange roughy, cut into 1/2-inch strips

2 tbsp. light mayonnaise

1/2 c. fat-free or light* sour cream

2 tbsp. lime juice

1/2 c. loosely packed cilantro, finely chopped

2 tsp. minced or chopped garlic

Salt and pepper to taste

1 10-oz. (280 g) package shredded cabbage

2 vine-ripened tomatoes

1 tsp. canola oil

Canola cooking spray

8 medium corn tortillas

Salsa Guacamole, if desired

1. In a medium bowl, mix the dry taco seasoning envelope with the amount of water indicated on the package. Add the fish pieces and stir to coat. Let the fish marinate until ready to cook. (A gallon-sized zip-top plastic bag can be used in place of a medium bowl.)
2. In a small bowl, combine the mayonnaise, sour cream, lime juice, cilantro, and garlic; stir well. Add salt and pepper to taste. Set aside.
3. In a large bowl, combine the shredded cabbage and tomatoes. Drizzle the sauce over the top and toss to blend well.
4. Spread 1 teaspoon of canola oil in large nonstick frying pan, and place over medium heat. When the pan is hot, add the fish. Spray the tops of the fish with canola cooking spray and cook for 3–4 minutes. Flip carefully with a spatula and cook for another 3–4 minutes, or until done.
5. In a medium nonstick frying pan, heat each corn tortilla until softened and warm. Set aside on a plate and cover with a dish towel to keep warm.
6. Assemble the fish tacos by laying each tortilla on a plate and dividing the fish, cabbage, and sauce among them. Top with Salsa Guacamole, if desired.

NUTRITIONAL ANALYSES (PER SERVING)

	BEFORE	AFTER		BEFORE	AFTER
CALORIES	940	346	CHOLESTEROL	120 MG	41 MG
PROTEIN	38 G	30 G	FIBER	4 G	6 G
CARBOHYDRATES	64 G	39 G	SODIUM	1320 MG	305 MG
FAT	58 G	8 G	% CALORIES FROM FAT	56	21
SATURATED FAT	16 G	1.3 G	OMEGA-3 FATTY ACIDS	N/A	0.7 G
MONOUNSATURATED FAT	N/A	1.9 G	OMEGA-6 FATTY ACIDS	N/A	1.2 G
POLYUNSATURATED FAT	N/A	2 G	*Nutritional analyses do not account for substitutions.		

Beer-Battered Fish

MAKES 4 SERVINGS

If you've ever had traditional fish-and-chips, you know they are a delicious but very greasy treat. This lighter version is great with malt vinegar and any of the fries in this book.

1 1/2 tbsp. canola oil
1 c. unbleached white flour
1/2 tsp. white pepper
1/2 tsp. seasoning salt
2/3 c. amber beer (nonalcoholic, if available)
2 egg whites, beaten to soft peaks
2 c. fine plain breadcrumbs (use French breadcrumbs, if available)

1 1/2 lb. (685 g) cod or orange roughy fillets (about 3/4 inch thick), cut crosswise into 1 1/2-inch-wide strips
Canola cooking spray
Malt vinegar, for serving
Chips or fries, for serving (optional)

1. Preheat the oven to 450° F (230° C). Coat the bottom of a jelly roll pan or cookie sheet with canola oil; set aside.
2. In a large deep bowl, combine the flour, white pepper, and seasoning salt, and stir together. Whisk in the beer. Gently fold in the egg whites; the batter will be light and fluffy. Spread out the breadcrumbs in a shallow medium-sized bowl.
3. Use a fork to dip a strip of fish into the batter, shaking off the excess. Then dip the fish into the breadcrumbs and shake off the excess. Place on the prepared pan. Repeat with the remaining fish strips, placing them on the prepared pan and making sure they don't touch. Spray the tops of the fish strips generously with canola cooking spray.
4. Bake for about 20 minutes or until the fish is cooked through and the crust is lightly browned. Transfer to a broiler about 6 inches from the heat and cook for 1–2 minutes or until the top is nicely crisp and brown. Serve with malt vinegar and chips or fries, if you'd like.

NUTRITIONAL ANALYSES (PER SERVING)

	BEFORE	AFTER		BEFORE	AFTER
CALORIES	444	328	CHOLESTEROL	64 MG	64 MG
PROTEIN	33 G	33 G	FIBER	1.5 G	1.5 G
CARBOHYDRATES	31 G	31 G	SODIUM	373 MG	373 MG
FAT	20 G	6 G	% CALORIES FROM FAT	41	16
SATURATED FAT	2.2 G	0.5 G	OMEGA-3 FATTY ACIDS	0.6 G	0.5 G
MONOUNSATURATED FAT	5.5 G	2.2 G	OMEGA-6 FATTY ACIDS	8.7 G	0.8 G
POLYUNSATURATED FAT	9.4 G	1.4 G			

Pistachio-Crusted Calamari
with **Lemon-Caper Sauce**
MAKES 4 SERVINGS

I am completely in love with a dish that a restaurant chain in California serves. This recipe is my attempt at reproducing it with a light twist. And I'm happy to announce that it still tastes delicious! We are pan-frying the squid steaks in a nonstick frying pan using a little bit of oil and coating the top of the steaks with canola cooking spray.

12–14 oz. (340–400 g) squid steaks, uncooked (about 4 steaks)
1/2 c. shelled pistachio nuts
1/4 c. panko crumbs
  (1/2 c. cornflakes can be substituted*)
1/4 tsp. salt
1/4 tsp. pepper

1/3 c. egg substitute
  (such as Egg Beaters)
2 tsp. canola oil
Canola cooking spray
Lemon wedges, for serving
Lemon-Caper Sauce (recipe follows),
  for serving

1. Rinse the squid steaks and pat dry with paper towels.
2. In the bowl of a food processor, combine the pistachios, panko crumbs, salt, and pepper, and pulse to process into fine crumbs. Transfer the mixture to a shallow, medium-sized bowl. Place the egg substitute in a separate medium-sized bowl.
3. Dip the squid steaks into the egg substitute, draining any excess, then into the pistachio-crumb mixture to coat well on both sides. Repeat with the remaining squid.
4. Place the canola oil in a large, nonstick frying pan or skillet over medium heat. Make sure the oil is nicely spread out over the bottom of the pan and add the coated squid steaks. Coat the tops with canola cooking spray.
5. Cook until the bottom of the squid is nicely golden, about 3 minutes, then use a spatula to flip the steaks. Cook the other side until golden, about 3 minutes more. Check the

NUTRITIONAL ANALYSES (PER SERVING)

	BEFORE	AFTER		BEFORE	AFTER
CALORIES	308	183	CHOLESTEROL	284 MG	231 MG
PROTEIN	21.5 G	19 G	FIBER	1.5 G	1.2 G
CARBOHYDRATES	13 G	8 G	SODIUM	342 MG	248 MG
FAT	19.5 G	8.3 G	% CALORIES FROM FAT	57	41
SATURATED FAT	3 G	1 G	OMEGA-3 FATTY ACIDS	0.6 G	0.8 G
MONOUNSATURATED FAT	6.7 G	4.1 G	OMEGA-6 FATTY ACIDS	7.7 G	1.9 G
POLYUNSATURATED FAT	8.3 G	2.7 G	*Nutritional analyses do not account for substitutions.		

thickest part of one of the steaks to make sure the squid is cooked through (it should be solid white and the same texture throughout).

6. Serve immediately with lemon wedges alongside and Lemon-Caper Sauce drizzled over the top.

Lemon-Caper Sauce

MAKES 4 SERVINGS

The original version of this recipe is more like a melted butter, so this version goes lighter on the butter and heavier on the lemon. Drizzled over the top of any fish, it's a tasty addition.

1 tbsp. butter
Juice of 1 lemon

2 tsp. capers in brine, drained

1. Place a small nonstick saucepan over medium heat. Add the butter and melt, stirring frequently, until the foamy stage is just past and the butter begins to brown (the butter will have a wonderful smell).
2. Stir in the juice from the lemon (discard any seeds) and the capers and continue to cook for a minute to blend the flavors. Remove from the heat and drizzle over the fish.

FRY LIGHT, FRY RIGHT PREPARATION (PER SERVING)

	BEFORE	AFTER		BEFORE	AFTER
CALORIES	106	28	CHOLESTEROL	31 MG	8 MG
PROTEIN	0.3 G	0.1 G	FIBER	0.5 G	0.1 G
CARBOHYDRATES	1.4 G	1.1 G	SODIUM	160 MG	72 MG
FAT	11.5 G	2.9 G	% CALORIES FROM FAT	94	93
SATURATED FAT	7.2 G	1.8 G	OMEGA-3 FATTY ACIDS	0 G	0.04 G
MONOUNSATURATED FAT	3.5 G	0.8 G	OMEGA-6 FATTY ACIDS	0.4 G	0.07 G
POLYUNSATURATED FAT	0.4 G	0.1 G			

Pan-Fried Trout with Lemon Slices

MAKES 6 SERVINGS

This could become a new campout favorite for your family. It's a spin on a traditional fish fry, where more oil, and even some butter, is normally called for —but this version uses a lot less fat. To help keep the fish moist and flavorful, place some lemon slices inside the trout and in the pan, and cover the fish during the second phase of cooking. This is especially good served with Skillet Potatoes (see page 117).

4 medium-sized trout (about 9 oz., or
    255 g, each), gutted and cleaned
    (preferably deboned)
1 tsp. salt, divided
1/2 tsp. pepper, divided

1/4 c. white flour
2 lemons, washed and cut into
    1/4-inch-thick slices
1 tbsp. olive oil
1/2 tsp. sesame oil

1. Rinse the trout and pat them very well dry. Combine 1/2 teaspoon of the salt, 1/4 teaspoon of the pepper, and the flour in a small bowl. Blend well with a fork, then pour onto a plate.
2. Season the inside of the trout with the remaining 1/2 teaspoon of salt and 1/4 teaspoon of pepper. Slide 2 slices of lemon into each trout cavity. Coat the outside of each trout in the flour mixture.
3. Place a large nonstick skillet over medium-high heat. Add the olive oil and sesame oil to the pan and stir with a spatula to coat the bottom well with both oils. Lay the lemon-stuffed trout into the pan and place the remaining lemon slices in any leftover space in the pan. Cook for about 5 minutes. Use a spatula to carefully flip the trout, then lay the lightly browned lemon slices on top of the cooked side of the trout. Cover the skillet and cook for about 5 minutes more (or until the trout is flaky and cooked through). Serve immediately.

NUTRITIONAL ANALYSES (PER SERVING)

	BEFORE	AFTER		BEFORE	AFTER
CALORIES	358	224	CHOLESTEROL	130 MG	89 MG
PROTEIN	32 G	32 G	FIBER	0.2 G	0.2 G
CARBOHYDRATES	5 G	5 G	SODIUM	580 MG	434 MG
FAT	23 G	8 G	% CALORIES FROM FAT	58	32
SATURATED FAT	11 G	1.5 G	OMEGA-3 FATTY ACIDS	1.3 G	1.1 G
MONOUNSATURATED FAT	8 G	3.5 G	OMEGA-6 FATTY ACIDS	1 G	0.7 G
POLYUNSATURATED FAT	2.6 G	2.1 G			

Prawns with Glazed Spiced Walnuts

MAKES 3 SERVINGS

This is one of the dishes people love to order in Chinese restaurants. But the prawns and walnuts are often deep-fried, and the sauce is so rich it can seem like it's made mostly of mayonnaise. For this light rendition, we are pan-frying the shrimp in a tiny bit of canola oil and making the sauce with lighter ingredients. I love the lightly browned shrimp with the crunchy glazed walnuts covered in a mild, creamy sauce. This is perfect served over steamed brown rice.

1 tsp. lemon juice
3 tbsp. fat-free sweetened condensed milk
1 1/2 tbsp. light or low-fat mayonnaise
1 1/2 tsp. sugar
1 tbsp. egg substitute (such as Egg Beaters)
1 10-oz. (280 g) bag frozen large prawns
   or jumbo shrimp, deveined and shelled

1/2 c. flour
1 tbsp. canola oil
Canola cooking spray
1/3 c. Glazed Spiced Walnuts, see page
   177 (toasted walnuts can be used
   in a pinch)
2 c. steamed brown or white rice

1. In a large mixing bowl, combine the lemon juice, sweetened condensed milk, mayonnaise, sugar, and egg substitute. Mix thoroughly and set aside.
2. If the prawns are raw, fill a large saucepan with water and bring to a rapid boil. Blanch the prawns in boiling water for 30 seconds. Remove from the water with a slotted spoon and drain on paper towels. (If the prawns are frozen, just defrost them and skip to step #3.)
3. Place the flour on a plate or in a bowl and dredge the prawns in it.
4. Place the canola oil in a large nonstick frying pan over medium heat. When the oil is hot, add the prawns to the pan. Spray the tops of the prawns with canola cooking spray. Once the bottoms are golden, flip the prawns with spatula. When the other sides are golden, remove the prawns and drain them on paper towels.
5. Add the hot prawns and pecans to the lemon-milk mixture and toss thoroughly to blend. Serve on a bed of steamed rice.

NUTRITIONAL ANALYSES (PER SERVING, INCLUDING WALNUTS AND 2/3 C. BROWN RICE)

	BEFORE	AFTER		BEFORE	AFTER
CALORIES	743	494	CHOLESTEROL	140 MG	138 MG
PROTEIN	27 G	27 G	FIBER	1.7 G	3.3 G
CARBOHYDRATES	66.5 G	58 G	SODIUM	240 MG	240 MG
FAT	41.5 G	16 G	% CALORIES FROM FAT	50	30
SATURATED FAT	5.2 G	1.6 G	OMEGA-3 FATTY ACIDS	0.5 G	1.5 G
MONOUNSATURATED FAT	10.5 G	4.2 G	OMEGA-6 FATTY ACIDS	10 G	5.5 G
POLYUNSATURATED FAT	22.8 G	7 G			

Oven-Baked Coconut Shrimp
with **Fresh Pineapple Salsa**

MAKES 5 SERVINGS

In this makeover of a deep-fried favorite, large shrimp are coated with a seasoned cornstarch mixture, dipped in a frothy egg white mixture, coated with shredded sweetened coconut, and baked in the oven until crisp. The tart and tasty Fresh Pineapple Salsa (recipe follows) is a perfect complement to the lightly browned, slightly sweet coconut shrimp.

28 large fresh shrimp (about 1 1/2 lb., or 685 g) peeled, deveined, tail intact (can use frozen)
Canola cooking spray
1/3 c. cornstarch

3/4 tsp. salt
1/2 tsp. ground cayenne pepper
3 large egg whites
1 1/2 c. flaked sweetened coconut

1. Preheat the oven to 400° F (200° C). Rinse the shrimp in cold water; drain well on paper towels until dry. Line a baking sheet with aluminum foil and coat the foil with canola cooking spray.
2. Combine the cornstarch, salt, and cayenne pepper in a shallow dish; stir with a whisk. Place the egg whites in a medium bowl and beat with an electric mixer at medium-high speed until frothy, about 2 minutes. Place the coconut in shallow dish.
3. Working with two shrimp at a time: dredge in the cornstarch mixture, dip in the egg white, then dredge in the coconut, gently pressing the coconut into the shrimp to coat. Place the shrimp on the prepared sheet, and repeat the dredging process with remaining shrimp.
4. Lightly coat the shrimp with canola cooking spray and bake for 10 minutes. Use a spatula to flip the shrimp and cook for 10 minutes more, or until the shrimp are cooked through. Serve immediately with Fresh Pineapple Salsa on the side.

NUTRITIONAL ANALYSES (PER SERVING)

	BEFORE	AFTER		BEFORE	AFTER
CALORIES	377	257	CHOLESTEROL	206 MG	206 MG
PROTEIN	31 G	31 G	FIBER	1 G	1 G
CARBOHYDRATES	16 G	16 G	SODIUM	621 MG	621 MG
FAT	20.6 G	7 G	% CALORIES FROM FAT	49	24
SATURATED FAT	5.4 G	4.7 G	OMEGA-3 FATTY ACIDS	0.8 G	0.7 G
MONOUNSATURATED FAT	3.9 G	0.6 G	OMEGA-6 FATTY ACIDS	8.1 G	0.2 G
POLYUNSATURATED FAT	9 G	1 G			

Fresh Pineapple Salsa

MAKES 1 2/3 C. (ABOUT 6 SERVINGS)

1 c. finely chopped fresh pineapple
1/3 c. finely chopped red onion
1/4 c. pineapple or apricot-pineapple
   preserves
1/4 c. chopped fresh cilantro

1 1/2 tbsp. fresh lime juice
1 tbsp. finely minced seeded jalapeño
   chili pepper
1/4 tsp. black pepper, to taste

Gently toss together the ingredients in a medium bowl. Serve immediately or cover and refrigerate for up to 3 days or until needed.

FRY LIGHT, FRY RIGHT PREPARATION (PER 1/4 C. SERVING)*

CALORIES	50	FIBER	1 G
PROTEIN	0.3 G	SODIUM	6 MG
CARBOHYDRATE	13 G	% CALORIES FROM FAT	0
FAT	0 G	OMEGA-3 FATTY ACIDS	0 G
SATURATED FAT	N/A	OMEGA-6 FATTY ACIDS	0 G
MONOUNSATURATED FAT	N/A		
POLYUNSATURATED FAT	N/A	*Nutritional analysis does not differ significantly
CHOLESTEROL	0 MG	from traditional preparation.

Perfected P. F. Chang's Shrimp Fried Rice

MAKES 2 LARGE SERVINGS

The shrimp fried rice at P. F. Chang's China Bistro is a personal favorite with nicely subtle flavors—but it could be lighter in the oil department. I was able to stir-fry this similar dish together using only 4 teaspoons of canola oil.

1/4 tsp. ground superfine mustard
1/4 tsp. minced fresh gingerroot
1/2 tsp. minced or crushed garlic
1 tsp. molasses
1 1/2 tbsp. lower-sodium soy sauce (serve more at the table, if desired)
Canola cooking spray
1 c. egg substitute (such as Egg Beaters)
Salt and pepper to taste

4 tsp. canola oil
1 1/2 c. packed, frozen, tail-off cooked large shrimp, partially defrosted
3/4 c. petite green peas, frozen, or 3/4 c. fresh bean sprouts
3/4 c. baby carrots, cut into matchsticks
2 c. steamed rice
2–3 green onions, whites or whites and greens, chopped

1. In a small bowl or cup, whisk together the mustard, gingeroot, garlic, and molasses. Whisk in the soy sauce and set aside.
2. Place a large, nonstick frying pan over medium heat. Spray the center generously with canola cooking spray. Pour the egg substitute into the middle of the pan and tilt to spread. Sprinkle salt and pepper over the top if desired. Once the underside is lightly browned, flip the egg over and cook for about a minute longer or until the bottom is lightly browned. Remove the egg from the pan, cut into small strips with a knife, and set aside.
3. Add the canola oil to the same pan and place over medium heat. Add the shrimp and let sizzle for about 1 minute. Add the peas and carrots and stir-fry for 2 minutes or until the shrimp is warmed through. Stir in the steamed rice and let cook for about 1 minute. Drizzle in the soy sauce mixture, stir, and let cook for 1–2 minutes. Turn off the heat and stir in the green onion and egg pieces.
4. Serve hot with additional soy sauce at the table, if desired.

NUTRITIONAL ANALYSES (PER SERVING)

	BEFORE	AFTER		BEFORE	AFTER
CALORIES	556	463	CHOLESTEROL	419 MG	207 MG
PROTEIN	36 G	36 G	FIBER	7 G	6 G
CARBOHYDRATES	55 G	55 G	SODIUM	915 MG	820 MG
FAT	20 G	11 G	% CALORIES FROM FAT	32	18
SATURATED FAT	3.7 G	1.2 G	OMEGA-3 FATTY ACIDS	0.5 G	1.3 G
MONOUNSATURATED FAT	5.5 G	6 G	OMEGA-6 FATTY ACIDS	8.9 G	2.3 G
POLYUNSATURATED FAT	9.4 G	3.6 G			

Chicken Flautas

MAKES 8 SERVINGS (3 FLAUTAS PER SERVING)

A typical deep-fried chicken flauta—tender seasoned chicken in a crispy tortilla shell—comes to around 990 calories and 75 grams of fat. But by oven-frying it and making a few ingredient adjustments, we can keep the same taste and texture and bring those numbers down to 380 calories and 10 grams of fat. Now, isn't that much better? I suggest serving these with guacamole, jalapeño jelly, or fat-free or light sour cream for dipping.

4 c. skinless boneless roast chicken or turkey breast, shredded

4 green onions, white and part of green, chopped

1 8-oz. (230 g) jar mild green taco sauce

1/4 tsp. ground cumin (optional)

8 oz. (230 g) shredded reduced-fat Monterey Jack cheese (or mixture of reduced-fat Colby and Jack)

24 medium corn tortillas

Canola cooking spray

1. Preheat the oven to 350° F (175° C). In a medium bowl, combine the shredded chicken, green onions, green taco sauce, cumin, and cheese. Mix together well.
2. Place a small, nonstick skillet over medium heat. Add a tortilla and let it heat for about a minute. Spray the top lightly with canola cooking spray and flip over; let it heat briefly. Place the now softened tortilla, sprayed-side down, in a 9- x 13-inch baking pan (you'll need two pans total).
3. Place 1/8 cup of chicken mixture in a line about a third of the way from one end of the tortilla. Wrap up the tortilla tightly, tucking in the ends, and place it seam-side down in the pan. Continue to heat up other tortillas while you fill softened tortillas with the chicken mixture.
4. Repeat steps #2 and #3 until all the tortillas are filled or the chicken mixture is used up—whichever comes first.
5. Bake for about 20–25 minutes or until the tortillas are a little crispy and golden brown. Serve the flautas with guacamole, jalapeño jelly, or fat-free or light sour cream for dipping.

NUTRITIONAL ANALYSES (PER 3 FLAUTAS)

	BEFORE	AFTER		BEFORE	AFTER
CALORIES	988	380	CHOLESTEROL	106 MG	80 MG
PROTEIN	39 G	34 G	FIBER	5 G	4.5 G
CARBOHYDRATES	37 G	39 G	SODIUM	598 MG	598 MG
FAT	76 G	10 G	% CALORIES FROM FAT	69	24
SATURATED FAT	12 G	5 G	OMEGA-3 FATTY ACIDS	1.9 G	0.1 G
MONOUNSATURATED FAT	32 G	1.4 G	OMEGA-6 FATTY ACIDS	25.7 G	1.3 G
POLYUNSATURATED FAT	27 G	1.4 G			

Finger-Lickin' Good Chicken

MAKES 4 SERVINGS

For this delectable, healthy take on fried chicken, we've marinated skinless pieces of white-meat chicken in low-fat buttermilk to make them tender, then coated them with a seasoned flour mixture and oven-fried them. A quick turn under the broiler makes the crust extra crispy. Serve with salad, corn on the cob, and mashed potatoes. This chicken is great cold, too!

4 boneless, skinless chicken breasts
1 c. low-fat buttermilk
2 tsp. canola oil
1 c. unbleached white flour
1/4 tsp. ground cumin

1 tsp. salt
1/2 tsp. ground chipotle or cayenne
   pepper, or more to taste
1/2 tsp. white pepper
Canola cooking spray

1. Place the chicken and buttermilk in a gallon-sized zip-top bag, seal the bag, and set in a medium-sized bowl in the refrigerator for several hours or overnight.
2. Preheat the oven to 450° F (230° C). Use a pastry brush to coat the bottom of a 9- x 9-inch baking dish with canola oil.
3. In a new gallon-sized zip-top bag or medium-sized shallow bowl, stir together the flour, cumin, salt, chipotle pepper, and white pepper to blend well.
4. Remove a piece of chicken from the buttermilk and gently shake off any excess. Immediately dip the chicken into the flour mixture and coat well. Holding the chicken over a plate, spray both sides well with canola cooking spray. Dip the chicken into the flour mixture a second time and spray again with canola cooking spray. Place in the prepared dish. Repeat with the remaining pieces of chicken.
5. Place the pan in the oven and bake until the chicken is cooked through and the coating is golden brown, about 25–30 minutes. Switch the oven to broil, and broil the chicken 6 inches from the heat for a minute or two (until the outside of the chicken is nicely browned), watching very carefully so as not to burn.

NUTRITIONAL ANALYSES (PER SERVING)

	BEFORE	AFTER		BEFORE	AFTER
CALORIES	470	194	CHOLESTEROL	160 MG	74 MG
PROTEIN	39 G	28 G	FIBER	1 G	0.2 G
CARBOHYDRATES	17 G	6 G	SODIUM	874 MG	225 MG
FAT	28 G	5.5 G	% CALORIES FROM FAT	54	25
SATURATED FAT	8 G	1 G	OMEGA-3 FATTY ACIDS	N/A	0.3 G
MONOUNSATURATED FAT	16.7 G	2.5 G	OMEGA-6 FATTY ACIDS	N/A	1 G
POLYUNSATURATED FAT	3.3 G	1.4 G			

Oven-Fried Lemon Marinated Chicken

MAKES 4 SERVINGS

This is a healthful version of that deep-fried lemon chicken many of us love to order at Chinese restaurants. This is truly a family favorite. Each serving can be accompanied by 3/4 cup steamed brown or white rice, if you wish.

1 tbsp. soy sauce
3/4 tsp. salt, divided
3/4 tsp. pepper, divided
1 1/2 tsp. minced garlic
   (or 2 cloves garlic, minced)
1 tbsp. canola oil
3 tbsp. condensed chicken broth
1/2 c. lemon juice

2 tbsp. grated lemon peel (wash lemon first)
4 skinless, boneless chicken breasts
Canola cooking spray
1/2 c. unbleached flour
   (plus more if needed)
1–2 tsp. paprika, to taste
Fresh parsley and lemon slices for
   garnish (optional)

1. Combine the soy sauce, 1/2 teaspoon of the salt, and 1/2 teaspoon of the pepper with the garlic, canola oil, broth, lemon juice, and lemon peel in a large zip-top plastic bag. Mix with a spoon; add the chicken breasts. Refrigerate for at least 1 hour.
2. Preheat the oven to 350° F (175° C). Coat a 9- x 9-inch pan with cooking spray and set aside.
3. Combine the flour, paprika, and remaining salt and pepper in a medium bowl or another plastic bag. Remove the chicken from the marinade, setting the marinade aside. Add the chicken to the flour mixture, coating each breast completely. Arrange the chicken in the prepared pan and spray the tops of the pieces with cooking spray.
4. Drizzle 1/4 cup of marinade over the chicken and bake for 20 minutes, uncovered. Pour the remaining marinade over the chicken and bake for 20–30 minutes more, until done. Garnish with lemon slices and fresh parsley if desired.

NUTRITIONAL ANALYSES (PER SERVING, WITHOUT RICE)

	BEFORE	AFTER		BEFORE	AFTER
CALORIES	320	200	CHOLESTEROL	68 MG	68 MG
PROTEIN	29 G	29 G	FIBER	3.5 G	3.5 G
CARBOHYDRATES	9 G	9 G	SODIUM	811 MG	811 MG
FAT	18.6 G	5 G	% CALORIES FROM FAT	52	22
SATURATED FAT	2.4 G	0.7 G	OMEGA-3 FATTY ACIDS	0.5 G	0.4 G
MONOUNSATURATED FAT	5.8 G	2.5 G	OMEGA-6 FATTY ACIDS	8.9 G	1 G
POLYUNSATURATED FAT	9.4 G	1.4 G			

Light Chicken Kiev

MAKES 4 SERVINGS

This is a light rendition of the famous Russian dish. Normally the chicken breasts are stuffed with a large knob of butter, breaded, and deep-fried. For this recipe, we're still stuffing with butter, but half as much, and we're still breading the chicken breast . . . but we're oven-frying instead of deep-frying. Serve with noodles or rice and steamed veggies or a nice green salad.

2 tbsp. butter (no- or low-trans-fat margarine can be substituted*), softened
1/4 tsp. ground black pepper
2 tsp. minced or chopped garlic (1/2 tsp. garlic powder can be substituted)
1 tbsp. finely chopped fresh parsley
4 skinless, boneless chicken breast halves (about 1.7 lb., or 650 g)
1 egg
2 tbsp. egg substitute (such as Egg Beaters)

2 tbsp. water
1/8 tsp. ground black pepper
1/4 tsp. garlic powder
1/2 tsp. dried dill weed
1/2 c. all-purpose flour
1/2 c. dry breadcrumbs (French or sourdough work well)
Canola cooking spray
Fresh parsley and lemon slices, for garnish (optional)

1. Combine the butter, 1/4 teaspoon black pepper, garlic, and parsley in a custard cup. On a 6- x 6-inch piece of aluminum foil, spread the mixture to about 2 x 3 inches. Place this mixture in the coldest section of your freezer and freeze until firm. This can be done ahead of time.
2. Remove and discard all fat from the chicken breasts. Place each chicken breast between two pieces of waxed paper and use a meat mallet to pound it to about 1/4 inch thick or less.
3. When the butter mixture is firm, remove from the freezer and cut into 6 equal pieces. Place 1 piece of butter on each chicken breast. Fold in the edges of the chicken and then roll (as you would an egg roll) to encase the butter completely. Secure the chicken rolls with small skewers or toothpicks.

4. In a mixing bowl, beat the egg, egg substitute, and water with an electric mixer until fluffy, about 2 minutes. In a separate bowl, mix the 1/8 teaspoon black pepper, 1/4 teaspoon garlic powder, dill weed, and flour. Place the breadcrumbs in a shallow bowl.
5. Coat the chicken well with the seasoned flour, dip into the egg mixture, and then roll in the breadcrumbs. Place the coated chicken on a shallow tray and chill in the refrigerator for 30 minutes.
6. Preheat the oven to 400° F (200° C). Cover a 9- x 9-inch baking dish with foil. Generously coat the outside of each chicken roll, all the way around, with canola cooking spray; place in the prepared dish. Bake until the chicken is cooked through and is golden brown on the outside, about 35 minutes (cut into one of the rolled chicken breasts to check). Transfer to the broiler and carefully broil the chicken for 1–2 minutes to brown the crumb coating a bit more.
7. Serve immediately, garnished with a sliced lemon twist and a sprinkling of parsley if desired. If there are some juices in the bottom of the dish, you can spoon them over the chicken before serving.

NUTRITIONAL ANALYSES (PER SERVING)

	BEFORE	AFTER		BEFORE	AFTER
CALORIES	538	255	CHOLESTEROL	202 MG	114 MG
PROTEIN	38 G	30 G	FIBER	0.5 G	0.5 G
CARBOHYDRATES	24 G	10 G	SODIUM	710 MG	210 MG
FAT	31 G	9.8 G	% CALORIES FROM FAT	52	35
SATURATED FAT	12.5 G	4.7 G	OMEGA-3 FATTY ACIDS	0.4 G	0.2 G
MONOUNSATURATED FAT	11.5 G	3.2 G	OMEGA-6 FATTY ACIDS	4.5 G	0.9 G
POLYUNSATURATED FAT	5 G	1.1 G			

*Nutritional analyses do not account for substitutions.

Chinese Sweet & Sour Chicken

MAKES 4 LARGE SERVINGS

There's something so satisfying about sweet-and-sour chicken—the play of sugar and acidity, the crispy fried batter and succulent meat. When Chinese restaurants prepare this dish, they often use skin-on thighs and drumstick meat. To keep the fat to a minimum, we are using skinless, boneless chicken breast or breast tenders. And instead of coating the chicken pieces in an egg batter, then deep-frying them in oil, we're coating them in egg, then in the flour mixture, then pan-frying them in a bit of canola oil. This trims the fat and calories big time!

1/2 c. unbleached or all-purpose flour
1/2 c. cornstarch
1/2 tsp. salt
1/4 tsp. ground white pepper
1 large egg
1 tbsp. water
1 lb. (454 g) chicken tenders, tendons removed, cut into bite-sized pieces and patted dry with paper towels

1 8-oz. (230 g) can pineapple chunks in juice (do not drain)
2/3 c. Heinz chili sauce
2/3 c. red currant jelly
1 c. celery hearts, sliced crosswise
1 green pepper, stemmed, seeded, quartered, and sliced into 1/4-inch-thick strips (about 1 1/4 c.)
1 tbsp. canola oil
Canola cooking spray

1. In a medium-sized, shallow bowl, combine the flour, cornstarch, salt, and pepper. Stir with a fork to blend well; set aside.
2. Place the egg and water in a small mixing bowl and beat with an electric mixer on medium speed until smooth. Add the chicken pieces, stir, and set aside.
3. Place a large saucepan over high heat and add the pineapple chunks (including juice), chili sauce, jelly, celery, and green pepper; bring to a boil. Reduce the heat to a simmer and cook for 10 minutes, uncovered, stirring occasionally.
4. While the sweet-and-sour sauce is simmering, place a large nonstick skillet over medium-high heat. Add the canola oil and spread evenly with a spatula.

5. Use a slotted spoon to remove about a third of the chicken pieces from the egg mixture (letting the excess drain off) and transfer to the flour mixture. Turn the pieces in the flour mixture to coat well, then carefully and quickly place the flour-coated chicken pieces in the hot oil in the pan. Repeat with the remaining chicken. Let the chicken pieces brown for about 4 minutes.

6. As the chicken browns on the bottom, generously coat the tops with canola cooking spray. Use a spatula to flip the chicken pieces to brown the other side, breaking the pieces apart from each other, if necessary. When the chicken is cooked through (about 3 more minutes), remove to the simmering sweet-and-sour sauce. Continue to cook, stirring frequently, for about 1–2 minutes to blend the flavors. Remove from the heat and serve over steamed rice.

NUTRITIONAL ANALYSES (PER SERVING, WITHOUT RICE)

	BEFORE	AFTER		BEFORE	AFTER
CALORIES	576	456	CHOLESTEROL	92 MG	92 MG
PROTEIN	29 G	29 G	FIBER	2 G	2 G
CARBOHYDRATES	72 G	72 G	SODIUM	883 MG	883 MG
FAT	19.5 G	6 G	% CALORIES FROM FAT	30	12
SATURATED FAT	10.3 G	8 G	OMEGA-3 FATTY ACIDS	0.6 G	0.6 G
MONOUNSATURATED FAT	8.8 G	2.6 G	OMEGA-6 FATTY ACIDS	5.1 G	0.8 G
POLYUNSATURATED FAT	5.8 G	1.5 G			

Chicken ruffs with
Orange Soy Dipping Sauce
MAKES 4 SERVINGS

This is a popular recipe on one of my favorite Web sites. Normally in this dish, the chicken pieces are battered and deep-fried. This version still uses a light batter, but the chicken puffs are pan-fried in a nonstick pan coated with a bit of canola oil. Please don't be intimidated by the number of ingredients. Most of them are for the Orange Soy Dipping Sauce, which is very quick to put together and is a wonderful complement for the chicken puffs. Serve with lots of veggies and brown or white rice.

3/4 c. orange juice

3/4 c. water

2/3 c. dark brown sugar

3 tbsp. rice vinegar

3 tbsp. lower-sodium soy sauce

2 tbsp. lemon juice

1 tsp. minced fresh ginger

1/2 tsp. minced or chopped garlic

1/4 tsp. crushed red pepper flakes (optional)

4 boneless, skinless chicken breasts,
    cut into large bite-sized pieces up to
    1 inch x 1 inch

5 tsp. cornstarch

3 tbsp. water

3/4 c. ice water

1 large egg

1/4 tsp. baking soda

1/4 tsp. salt

1 1/2 c. unsifted cake flour (regular flour
    can be substituted), divided

2 tbsp. canola oil, or more if necessary

Canola cooking spray

1. Place all the ingredients through the crushed red pepper flakes in a small nonstick saucepan over high heat. Stir often as you bring the mixture to a boil; when the mixture reaches a boil, remove it from the heat and let it cool in the pan, uncovered.
2. Place 1 cup of the orange glaze mixture and the chicken pieces in a bowl or plastic freezer bag and refrigerate for at least 2 hours or up to 12 hours. (If you are in a hurry, you can skip the marination process and proceed to the next step.)
3. Combine the cornstarch with 3 tablespoons of water in a small bowl and stir until the cornstarch is dissolved. Add this mixture to the sauce in the pan and stir well. Place the

sauce over medium-high heat, stirring frequently, until the sauce begins to thicken (2–3 minutes). Cover the pan and remove from the heat.

4. To make the batter: In a mixing bowl using an electric mixer at medium speed, beat together the ice water and egg, then beat in the baking soda and salt. Add in 3/4 cup of the flour and beat on low for about 6 seconds. In two batches, sprinkle another 1/4 cup of flour over the top of batter and stir briefly to blend. Place the remaining 1/2 cup of flour in a small bowl.

5. Place a large, nonstick frying pan or skillet over medium-high heat. Coat the bottom with about 1 tablespoon of the canola oil.

6. Place a handful of chicken pieces into the flour and coat well, then add them to the batter. Use a slotted spoon to remove the chicken from the batter, letting any excess batter drain off, and add them individually to the oil in the hot pan. Repeat until the pan is full (about half the chicken pieces). Spray the tops of the chicken pieces with canola cooking spray. When the bottoms are nicely browned and crispy (about 4 minutes), flip the chicken (a fork works well) and brown the other side—about 3–4 minutes. Repeat with the remaining chicken and oil.

7. Remove from the heat and serve immediately with the Orange Soy Dipping Sauce (the sauce can be warmed or served cold).

NUTRITIONAL ANALYSES (PER SERVING, IF ALL THE SAUCE IS CONSUMED)

	BEFORE	AFTER		BEFORE	AFTER
CALORIES	750	452	CHOLESTEROL	172 MG	121 MG
PROTEIN	39 G	31 G	FIBER	1 G	1 G
CARBOHYDRATES	69 G	59 G	SODIUM	1189 MG	615 MG
FAT	34 G	10 G	% CALORIES FROM FAT	41	20
SATURATED FAT	7.1 G	1.3 G	OMEGA-3 FATTY ACIDS	0.4 G	0.7 G
MONOUNSATURATED FAT	11.5 G	5 G	OMEGA-6 FATTY ACIDS	12.1 G	1.9 G
POLYUNSATURATED FAT	12.5 G	2.7 G			

Chicken-Fried Steak
with Country Gravy

MAKES 4 SERVINGS

This dish may hail from the South, but today people all over the United States enjoy chicken-fried steak. You may be surprised to know that naturally extra-lean cube steaks are the typical cut of choice for this dish. So let's keep it lean by pan-frying the breaded steaks in a little bit of canola oil instead of submerging them in fat and deep-frying them. These are delicious with light mashed potatoes (made with fat-free half-and-half or lowfat-milk) or rice.

1/4 tsp. salt (optional)

1/2 tsp. black pepper, divided

4 cube steaks (about 1 1/3 lb., or 600 g)

1 large egg

1/4 c. egg substitute (such as Egg Beaters)

1 1/4 c. fat-free half-and-half (evaporated skimmed milk can be substituted), divided

1 c. plus 2 tbsp. unbleached white flour, divided

1/2 tsp. ground red pepper (optional)

1 c. seasoned or plain breadcrumbs, or crushed saltine crackers

1 tbsp. canola oil

Canola cooking spray

2 tbsp. Wondra quick-mixing flour

1 c. low-fat milk

Chopped fresh parsley, for garnish (optional)

1. Sprinkle the salt and 1/4 tsp. pepper evenly over the steaks. Set aside.
2. In a small bowl, beat together the egg, egg substitute, and 1/4 cup of the half-and-half. In a medium-sized bowl, combine the 1 cup of the flour with remaining 1/4 tsp. pepper and 1/2 teaspoon ground red pepper; blend with a fork. Place the breadcrumbs in a separate bowl.
3. Place the canola oil in a large, heavy, nonstick skillet over medium-high heat. Once it's hot, tilt the pan to coat the bottom evenly. Meanwhile, dip both sides of each cube steak in the flour mixture, then the egg mixture, and finally into the breadcrumbs, coating well.
4. When the oil is very hot, add the steaks to the skillet. Spray the tops with canola cooking spray and cook for about 4 minutes, or until golden brown on the bottom.

5. Flip the steaks over to brown the other side (about 4 minutes). Turn off the heat, remove the steaks to a baking pan, and keep warm in a 200° F (90° C) oven—don't clean the skillet yet.
6. To make the gravy, combine 1/4 cup of the half-and-half with the Wondra in a bowl and stir to make a paste. Slowly whisk in the remaining 3/4 cup of half-and-half, along with the low-fat milk. Start heating the skillet (the one the steaks were just in) over low heat. Pour the gravy mixture into the hot skillet and loosen the browned bits from the bottom of the pan with a wooden spoon. Continue to stir and cook until the gravy has thickened to your liking (I usually cook about 2–3 minutes). Add salt and pepper to taste.
7. Serve each chicken-fried steak with light mashed potatoes or rice, a wonderful spoon of country gravy over the top, and some chopped fresh parsley.

NUTRITIONAL ANALYSES (PER SERVING WITH GRAVY)

	BEFORE	AFTER		BEFORE	AFTER
CALORIES	650	433	CHOLESTEROL	150 MG	135 MG
PROTEIN	20 G	52 G	FIBER	1 G	1 G
CARBOHYDRATES	50 G	24 G	SODIUM	2260 MG	259 MG
FAT	37 G	12 G	% CALORIES FROM FAT	51	25
SATURATED FAT	13 G	3.5 G	OMEGA-3 FATTY ACIDS	N/A	0.4 G
MONOUNSATURATED FAT	N/A	5.3 G	OMEGA-6 FATTY ACIDS	N/A	1 G
POLYUNSATURATED FAT	N/A	1.4 G			

Homestyle Steak Fajitas with Salsa Guacamole

MAKES 6 FAJITAS

This fajita-meat marinade and sauce contains almost no fat and is quick to prepare, too. The meat and veggies in fajitas are often pan-fried in oil, so to make this recipe healthier we're pan-frying them in the fajita sauce instead. I like my fajitas on the nonspicy side, but "some like it hot"—so I added some fiery options.

1 lb. (454 g) round steak or skirt steak (trimmed of visible fat) or skinless, boneless chicken breast

1 c. condensed reduced-sodium chicken broth

2 tbsp. lower-sodium soy sauce

2 tsp. Worcestershire sauce

1 1/2 tsp. minced or chopped garlic

1/2 tsp. black pepper

2 tsp. lemon juice

1 tbsp. maple syrup (reduced-calorie pancake syrup can be substituted*)

1/2–1 tsp. red pepper flakes (optional)

1 recipe Salsa Guacamole (recipe follows)

1 onion, cut in half, each half cut into slices

1 bell pepper, top removed, cut in half, and each half cut into slices

1–2 tbsp. chopped seeded jalapeño pepper (optional)

6 fajita- or soft-taco-style white or whole wheat flour tortillas

3 c. shredded lettuce

1. Cut the meat into 1/4-inch-thick strips. In a medium-sized bowl, combine the marinade ingredients through the red pepper flakes. Add the meat strips to the bowl, cover, and refrigerate for 4 hours. (If you don't have the time, you can skip the refrigeration and go straight to step #2.)
2. Prepare the Salsa Guacamole and keep covered in the refrigerator in a serving bowl.
3. Place a large nonstick skillet over medium-high heat. Pour the meat and marinade into the skillet, add the onion, bell pepper, and jalapeño, and continue cooking, stirring occasionally, until most of the marinade has boiled off.

NUTRITIONAL ANALYSES (PER FAJITA, NOT INCLUDING SALSA GUACAMOLE)

	BEFORE	AFTER		BEFORE	AFTER
CALORIES	399	279	CHOLESTEROL	45 MG	33 MG
PROTEIN	22.6 G	21 G	FIBER	2 G	2 G
CARBOHYDRATES	35.6 G	35.5 G	SODIUM	727 MG	727 MG
FAT	18.2 G	6 G	% CALORIES FROM FAT	41	19
SATURATED FAT	5.5 G	1.3 G	OMEGA-3 FATTY ACIDS	0.3 G	0.4 G
MONOUNSATURATED FAT	7.6 G	2.5 G	OMEGA-6 FATTY ACIDS	3.1 G	0.4 G
POLYUNSATURATED FAT	3.5 G	0.8 G	* Nutritional analyses do not account for substitutions.		

4. Soften the tortillas by placing them in the microwave and heating on high for 1 minute (or heat in nonstick frying pan over medium heat until soft or light brown).
5. To assemble the fajitas, spoon some of the meat-onion mixture into each tortilla. Top with shredded lettuce and Salsa Guacamole.

Salsa Guacamole

MAKES 6 SERVINGS

This marriage of salsa and guacamole creates a creamy yet zesty sauce—perfect with homemade fajitas.

1 whole avocado, peeled, pitted, and roughly chopped
1 tbsp. taco sauce or salsa (mild or hot, to taste)

3 tbsp. fat-free sour cream or low-fat plain yogurt*
1/2 c. chopped tomatoes
Dried red pepper flakes or finely chopped jalapeño, to taste (for added heat)

Combine the avocado, taco sauce, and sour cream in the bowl of a food processor and pulse until smooth. Stir in the chopped tomatoes and pepper flakes or jalapeño to taste. Serve immediately, or cover and refrigerate for up to 24 hours or until needed.

FRY LIGHT, FRY RIGHT PREPARATION (PER SERVING)**

CALORIES	65	FIBER	2 G
PROTEIN	1.2 G	SODIUM	28 MG
CARBOHYDRATE	4.6 G	% CALORIES FROM FAT	73
FAT	5 G	OMEGA-3 FATTY ACIDS	0.04 G
SATURATED FAT	0.9 G	OMEGA-6 FATTY ACIDS	0.6 G
MONOUNSATURATED FAT	3.2 G		
POLYUNSATURATED FAT	0.7 G	*Nutritional analyses do not account for substitutions.	
CHOLESTEROL	0.7 MG	**Nutritional analysis does not differ significantly from traditional preparation.	

Crispy Beef & Bean Tacos

MAKES 6 SERVINGS (2 TACOS PER SERVING)

Obviously, we could all eat soft tacos and skip the deep-fried tortillas that come with crispy tacos . . . but that would be no fun! In this recipe, we make crunchy corn tortillas by heating them in a nonstick frying pan, shaping them into taco shells, and then baking them.

1 lb. (454 g) superlean ground beef (or ground sirloin)
1 1-oz. (30 g) packet taco spices and seasonings (Lawry's brand is good)
2/3 c. water
1 15-oz. (425 g) can kidney beans, rinsed and drained

12 corn tortillas
Canola cooking spray
1 c. grated reduced-fat sharp cheddar cheese
6 c. shredded iceberg lettuce (other lettuce types can be used), divided
1 1/2 c. chopped tomatoes
Fresh or bottled salsa as desired

1. Preheat the oven to 300° F (150° C). In large nonstick skillet or frying pan over medium-high heat, brown the beef and break it up with a wooden spoon until crumbly. Add the taco seasoning packet, water, and beans; mix thoroughly.
2. Bring the beef mixture to a boil; reduce the heat to low and cook, uncovered, for about 6 minutes, stirring occasionally. Remove from the heat and cover to keep warm. (This makes enough beef-bean mixture for about 12 tacos.)
3. Place a medium, nonstick frying pan over medium-high heat. Spray one side of a corn tortilla with canola cooking spray and set in the hot pan, spray-side down. Spray the top with more canola cooking spray. After 1 minute, flip the tortilla and heat the other side for 1 minute more. Remove the tortilla from the pan, shape into a taco shell, and place on a jelly roll pan. Repeat with the remaining tortillas; when all are on the jelly roll pan, place it in the oven and bake until taco shells are crispy, about 15–20 minutes.
4. Remove the taco shells from the oven and divide the beef-bean mixture among them. Top with grated cheese, shredded lettuce, chopped tomatoes, and fresh or bottled salsa as desired.

NUTRITIONAL ANALYSES (PER SERVING, INCLUDING 1 TBSP. SALSA)

	BEFORE	AFTER		BEFORE	AFTER
CALORIES	440	354	CHOLESTEROL	53 MG	53 MG
PROTEIN	20 G	28 G	FIBER	6 G	9 G
CARBOHYDRATES	28 G	44 G	SODIUM	700 MG	475 MG
FAT	28 G	9 G	% CALORIES FROM FAT	57	23
SATURATED FAT	14 G	4 G	OMEGA-3 FATTY ACIDS	N/A	0.2 G
MONOUNSATURATED FAT	N/A	1.7 G	OMEGA-6 FATTY ACIDS	N/A	0.7 G
POLYUNSATURATED FAT	N/A	1.1 G			

Beef Flautas

MAKES 6 LONG FLAUTAS

In Spanish, flauta means "flute." Extra-long flautas, often sold by street vendors in Mexico, are made by overlapping two tortillas end to end. They are traditionally deep-fried, but here we're baking them instead. Flautas are fun to eat but can be messy, so wrap one end in foil and eat from the other to keep the filling from spilling out.

Canola cooking spray
1 lb. (454 g) extra-lean ground beef
2/3 c. chopped onion
1 tsp. minced or chopped garlic
1 1/2 tsp. chili powder
1 tsp. dried oregano
1/2 tsp. paprika

1/4 tsp. ground cumin
1/4 tsp. pepper
2 tsp. Worcestershire sauce
1/2 c. mild chili sauce (or canned tomato sauce)
12 medium corn tortillas
Mild salsa, fat-free or light sour cream,
    and guacamole, for serving

1. Preheat the oven to 400° F (200° C). Coat a large nonstick skillet with canola cooking spray and place over medium-high heat. Add the ground beef, onion, and garlic, and brown. Crumble the meat into small pieces, using a spatula, as it cooks.
2. Add the chili powder, oregano, paprika, cumin, pepper, Worcestershire sauce, and chili sauce. Stir well.
3. Place six corn tortillas in a damp kitchen towel and warm them in the microwave on medium for about 2 minutes. (Or heat one tortilla at a time in an ungreased frying pan over medium heat until flexible, about 15 seconds per side.)
4. For each flauta, lightly spray both sides of two tortillas with canola cooking spray. Lay the tortillas down so they overlap by 4 inches. Spoon 1/4 cup of filling down one side of the paired tortillas and roll up tightly, keeping the beef mixture in the center. Place seam-side down on a thick cookie sheet.
5. Bake the flautas in the preheated oven until the tortillas are crisp, about 15 minutes. Serve with salsa, fat-free sour cream, and guacamole, if desired.

NUTRITIONAL ANALYSES (PER FLAUTA)

	BEFORE	AFTER		BEFORE	AFTER
CALORIES	707	237	CHOLESTEROL	73 MG	40 MG
PROTEIN	27 G	18 G	FIBER	3.5 G	3 G
CARBOHYDRATES	27 G	33 G	SODIUM	780 MG	780 MG
FAT	55 G	5 G	% CALORIES FROM FAT	70	19
SATURATED FAT	9.5 G	1.5 G	OMEGA-3 FATTY ACIDS	1.3 G	0.2 G
MONOUNSATURATED FAT	23.5 G	1.7 G	OMEGA-6 FATTY ACIDS	17.5 G	0.6 G
POLYUNSATURATED FAT	18.8 G	1 G			

Light Beef Tostadas

MAKES 4 TOSTADAS

By baking the tortillas and using lower-fat key ingredients, these tostadas are a great light meal option!

4 corn tortillas (9 inches in diameter)
Canola cooking spray
12 oz. (340 g) ground sirloin or
    extra-lean beef
2/3 c. chopped onion
1 tsp. minced or pressed garlic
1 1/2 tsp. chili powder
1 tsp. paprika
1 tsp. dried oregano
1/4 tsp. ground cumin

1/4 tsp. black pepper (or to taste)
1/2 c. taco sauce or mild chili sauce
2 tsp. Worcestershire sauce
1 c. fat-free canned refried beans
1 c. shredded reduced-fat Monterey Jack
    or cheddar cheese
4 c. shredded lettuce
2 large or 3 medium tomatoes, chopped
Nonfat sour cream, chopped green onions,
    mild or hot salsa, for garnish (optional)

1. Preheat the oven to 300° F (150° C). Lightly coat the tortillas with canola cooking spray, then lay them on a nonstick baking sheet and bake until crisp, about 20 minutes. (The tortillas can also be toasted individually in a dry nonstick frying pan over medium heat, flipping often, until crisp, about 5 minutes.)
2. Place a large, nonstick frying pan over medium-high heat and add the ground beef, onion, and garlic. Crumble the beef into small pieces by pressing with a potato masher while it cooks. When the meat is browned and cooked through, stir in the remaining seasonings through the Worcestershire sauce and simmer on low until thickened, about 1 minute.
3. Place the beans in a small, microwave-safe covered bowl and heat on high for 2 minutes (or warm in a small saucepan over low heat).
4. Assemble the tostadas by dividing the crisp tortillas among dinner plates and topping each with layers of beans, beef, cheese, lettuce, tomato, and any of the optional garnishes.

NUTRITIONAL ANALYSES (PER TOSTADA)

	BEFORE	AFTER		BEFORE	AFTER
CALORIES	499	398	CHOLESTEROL	111 MG	50 MG
PROTEIN	24 G	32 G	FIBER	6 G	7 G
CARBOHYDRATES	45 G	36 G	SODIUM	1306 MG	796 MG
FAT	25.5 G	13.5 G	% CALORIES FROM FAT	46	31
SATURATED FAT	17.2 G	7 G	OMEGA-3 FATTY ACIDS	0.1 G	0.1 G
MONOUNSATURATED FAT	5.3 G	3.5 G	OMEGA-6 FATTY ACIDS	0.8 G	0.5 G
POLYUNSATURATED FAT	9 G	0.9 G			

Honey-Ginger–Glazed Spicy Crispy Beef

MAKES 4 SERVINGS

This is one of those recipes you want to make over and over again. It's lovely served with brown rice and green beans.

4 tbsp. lower-sodium soy sauce
1 tbsp. rice vinegar
1/2 tbsp. rice wine
1 1/2 tbsp. honey
7 tbsp. granulated sugar
1/2 tbsp. chili paste (for example, Thai Kitchen's Roasted Red Chili Paste)
1/4 c. water
3 tbsp. chopped fresh gingerroot
1/4 c. cornstarch

1/4 tsp. salt
1/4 tsp. black pepper
12 oz. (340 g) flank steak, trimmed of any visible fat and sliced about 1/4 inch thick
4 tsp. canola oil
Canola cooking spray
2 tsp. minced garlic
1/3 c. sliced onion
1/3 c. diced red bell pepper

1. In a small mixing bowl, combine the soy sauce, rice vinegar, rice wine, and honey. Add the sugar, chili paste, water, and gingerroot. Mix well and set aside.
2. In a large mixing bowl or gallon freezer bag, combine the cornstarch, salt, and pepper; mix thoroughly. Toss the steak slices in the cornstarch mixture and coat well.
3. Place a large, nonstick skillet over medium-high heat and add 4 teaspoons of canola oil to the bottom of the pan; tilt the skillet to coat the bottom well with oil. Add the coated steak slices and pan-fry until golden brown on both sides, about 5–6 minutes a side. Check to make sure they are cooked to your liking. Remove from the skillet and set aside.
4. Spray the skillet generously with canola cooking spray. Add the garlic, onion, and red pepper, and quickly sauté for 30 seconds. Add the soy sauce mixture, and cook for another 30 seconds. Finally, add the strips of fried steak back to the skillet and toss to heat through and coat with sauce. Serve immediately with rice, if desired.

NUTRITIONAL ANALYSES (PER SERVING)

	BEFORE	AFTER		BEFORE	AFTER
CALORIES	467	347	CHOLESTEROL	45 MG	45 MG
PROTEIN	19 G	19 G	FIBER	1.3 G	1.3 G
CARBOHYDRATES	38 G	38 G	SODIUM	650 M	650 M
FAT	26.6 G	13 G	% CALORIES FROM FAT	51	34
SATURATED FAT	7.1 G	4 G	OMEGA-3 FATTY ACIDS	0.6 G	0.5 G
MONOUNSATURATED FAT	9.5 G	6.2 G	OMEGA-6 FATTY ACIDS	9.1 G	1.2 G
POLYUNSATURATED FAT	9.7 G	1.7 G			

Pork Chimichangas with Lime-Cilantro Sauce

MAKES 9 CHIMICHANGAS

These flavorful chimichangas are a great variation for burrito night! And using the oven-frying method keeps them healthful—but still crispy on the outside. Instead of deep-frying these the traditional way, we're lightly brushing them with canola oil and oven-baking them until brown and toasty on the outside. You can freeze these in zippered freezer bags and reheat in a toaster oven for a quick dinner or lunch.

1 tbsp. canola oil

1 1/2 lb. (685 g) pork tenderloin (about 2 small tenderloins—available in supermarkets in vacuum-sealed packs), cut into 1-inch chunks

3 c. beef broth (lower sodium, if available)

2 tbsp. rice vinegar or distilled white vinegar

1/3 c. chopped green onions

1/3 c. finely chopped seeded moderate chili peppers (such as pasilla)

3 garlic cloves, minced (about 1/2 tbsp.)

1 tsp. dried oregano, crumbled

1/2 tsp. ground cumin

1 tbsp. canola oil (more if needed)

About 9 home-style flour tortillas (baby burrito size works great)

1 1/4 c. vegetarian or nonfat canned refried beans

Lime-Cilantro Sauce (recipe follows) and/or salsa of your choice, for serving

1. Spread the canola oil in the bottom of a large nonstick saucepan or skillet and place over medium-high heat. Add the pork and brown on all sides, 8–10 minutes.
2. Meanwhile, place the beef broth in a medium saucepan over medium heat. When the pork tenderloins are nicely browned, transfer the hot broth to the saucepan in which the pork is cooking, scraping the bottom of the pan with a wooden spoon to loosen any browned bits. Bring to a boil, then reduce the heat to low. Cover and simmer until the meat is tender, about 30–45 minutes.

3. Preheat the oven to 450° F (230° C). Uncover the saucepan, raise heat to high, and boil until more than half of broth has evaporated, 8–10 minutes. Add the vinegar, green onions, chili peppers, garlic, oregano, and cumin. Stir well and continue cooking until almost all of the broth has evaporated, about 5 minutes more. Let the pork cool completely, then shred using a spatula or large spoon.

4. Place a tablespoon of canola oil in a small dish and set aside a pastry brush. Place a tortilla in a large nonstick skillet over medium heat. When it's soft, flip the tortilla and brush its top with canola oil. Quickly flip the tortilla, oiled-side down, into a 9- x 13-inch baking dish. Spread 1/8 cup of refried beans in the center of the tortilla (to make a rectangle about 3 x 4 inches). Top with 1/4 cup of pork mixture. Fold in the sides and roll into a small, compact burrito. Place seam-side down in the 9- x 13-inch baking dish. Repeat with the remaining tortillas and filling.

5. Bake in the center of the oven for about 20 minutes or until both sides of chimichangas are nicely brown and crisp. Serve with Lime-Cilantro Sauce and/or salsa alongside.

NUTRITIONAL ANALYSES (PER CHIMICHANGA)

	BEFORE	AFTER		BEFORE	AFTER
CALORIES	768	333	CHOLESTEROL	89 MG	53 MG
PROTEIN	37 G	25 G	FIBER	N/A	3 G
CARBOHYDRATES	62 G	32 G	SODIUM	1356 MG	443 MG
FAT	43 G	11 G	% CALORIES FROM FAT	50	30
SATURATED FAT	18 G	2.4 G	OMEGA-3 FATTY ACIDS	N/A	0.4 G
MONOUNSATURATED FAT	N/A	5.4 G	OMEGA-6 FATTY ACIDS	N/A	1.5 G
POLYUNSATURATED FAT	N/A	2 G			

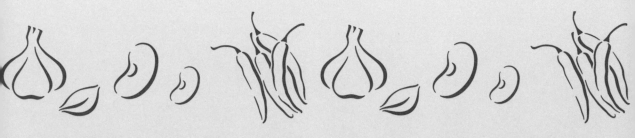

Lime-Cilantro Sauce

MAKES 1 1/2 C. (ABOUT 12 SERVINGS)

1 c. nonfat or light sour cream   1/2 c. chopped fresh cilantro
1/2 c. diced peeled and seeded cucumber   1 tbsp. fresh lime juice

Blend all the ingredients in a food processor, pulsing until the cucumber is finely chopped and a nice sauce has formed. Season with salt and pepper if desired. Transfer to a serving bowl. You can prepare this an hour ahead; just keep it covered in the refrigerator until needed.

FRY LIGHT, FRY RIGHT PREPARATION (PER 1/8 C.)*

CALORIES	21	SODIUM	16 MG
PROTEIN	1 G	% CALORIES FROM FAT	13
CARBOHYDRATE	3.5 G	OMEGA-3 FATTY ACIDS	0 G
FAT	0.3 G	OMEGA-6 FATTY ACIDS	0 G
SATURATED FAT	0.2 G		
MONOUNSATURATED FAT	0 G	*Nutritional analysis does not differ significantly
POLYUNSATURATED FAT	0 G	from traditional preparation.
CHOLESTEROL	2 MG	
FIBER	0.1 G	

Garlicky Thai Pork Stir-Fry

MAKES 4 SERVINGS

The trouble with many American stir-fry recipes is that they use far more oil than is actually necessary. This is a spicy and fragrant pork-and-veggie dish that uses the smallest amount of canola oil needed to pull it off. It is wonderful served over steamed brown or white rice.

4 tbsp. lower-sodium soy sauce
1 1/2 tbsp. honey
2 tsp. minced or chopped garlic
1/4 tsp. dried crushed red pepper
1 lb. (454 g) pork tenderloin, sliced into strips about 1/4 inch thick
3 tsp. canola oil
3 c. fresh or frozen green beans (if using fresh, remove ends and cut into 1 1/2-inch pieces)

1 large red bell pepper, cut into 1/4-inch-thick strips
1 tbsp. bottled or fresh minced ginger
Salt, to taste (optional)
Pepper, to taste
1/3 c. thinly sliced green onions, white and part of green, for garnish
1/4 c. finely chopped unsalted roasted peanuts (lightly salted peanuts can be substituted*) for garnish

1. Place the soy sauce, honey, garlic, and crushed red pepper in a medium-sized bowl and stir to blend well. Stir in the pork strips and set aside.
2. Add the canola oil to a nonstick wok or large nonstick skillet or frying pan over high heat. Add the pork mixture, green beans, bell pepper, and ginger and stir-fry until the pork is cooked through and the green beans are just tender, about 5 minutes.
3. Add salt, if desired, and pepper to taste and remove from the heat. Spoon onto individual plates and top each with a sprinkling of green onions and chopped peanuts.

NUTRITIONAL ANALYSES (PER SERVING)

	BEFORE	AFTER		BEFORE	AFTER
CALORIES	604	309	CHOLESTEROL	74 MG	79 MG
PROTEIN	33 G	31 G	FIBER	5 G	5 G
CARBOHYDRATES	40 G	17 G	SODIUM	1067 MG	562 MG
FAT	35 G	13 G	% CALORIES FROM FAT	52	37
SATURATED FAT	10.3 G	2.7 G	OMEGA-3	0.2 G	0.4 G
MONOUNSATURATED FAT	13.7 G	6.3 G	OMEGA-6	7.8 G	2.3 G
POLYUNSATURATED FAT	8.1 G	2.8 G	* Nutritional analyses do not account for substitutions.		

Faux Fast Food

In-a-Pinch Baked Pizza Pockets

MAKES 4 PIZZA POCKETS

Hot Pockets, a favorite item in the frozen-food aisle, are popular with kids and adults alike. But even their "lean" versions contain hydrogenated oils and are loaded with ingredients you can't pronounce. Our pizza pockets lighten things up and are healthier, too—they're lower in calories and lower in fat because they're made with bread dough and baked with only a brushing of olive oil.

1/4 c. shredded part-skim mozzarella cheese
1/4 c. shredded reduced-fat sharp cheddar
  cheese
1 11.3-oz. (320 g) can traditional dinner rolls
  (such as Pillsbury), divided into 8 rolls
4 tbsp. bottled pizza sauce or marinara sauce

Assorted finely chopped toppings—
  green onions, green peppers, lower-fat
  pepperoni, for example (optional)
1 tsp. olive oil
Mrs. Dash Garlic & Herb blend or
  any other favorite herb blend, to taste

1. Preheat the oven to 425° F (215° C). Place the cheeses in a small bowl and toss to blend well; set aside.
2. Roll each of the eight pieces of dough into as flat a circle as possible—about 3 1/2 to 4 inches in diameter.
3. Spoon 1 tablespoon of the pizza sauce onto four of the circles and spread, leaving a 1/3-inch rim around the edge.
4. Sprinkle about 2 tablespoons of the cheese mixture evenly over each of the sauce-topped circles. Add any assorted finely chopped toppings you like.
5. Lay the remaining four circles carefully over the topped circles (try to match the edges well), and use the tines of a fork to seal the edges together.
6. Brush the tops lightly with olive oil, then place the pizza pockets olive-oil-side down on a nonstick baking sheet. Brush the tops lightly with olive oil and sprinkle lightly with your desired herb blend.
7. Bake until golden brown and the crust is cooked through, about 18 minutes.

NUTRITIONAL ANALYSES (PER SERVING)

	BEFORE	AFTER		BEFORE	AFTER
CALORIES	370	228	CHOLESTEROL	41 MG	9 MG
PROTEIN	14 G	9 G	FIBER	1.5 G	1 G
CARBOHYDRATE	39 G	30 G	SODIUM	676 MG	474 MG
FAT	18 G	8 G	CALORIES FROM FAT	44	32
SATURATED FAT	7 G	3 G	OMEGA-3 FATTY ACIDS	N/A	0.2 G
MONOUNSATURATED FAT	6.5 G	3.3 G	OMEGA-6 FATTY ACIDS	N/A	0.6 G
POLYUNSATURATED FAT	2 G	0.8 G			

Crumb-Coated Baked Onion Rings

MAKES 8 SIDE SERVINGS

A serving of these freshly made onion rings contains 75 percent less fat and 60 percent fewer calories than a serving of onion rings from Jack in the Box. Using herb-seasoned fat-free crouton crumbs adds texture and flavor to the outside of your onion rings without adding hassle.

4 medium yellow or sweet onions
1 c. all-purpose flour
1 c. light or nonalcoholic beer
1/4 tsp. ground cayenne pepper
1/2 tsp. seasoning salt
1/4 tsp. freshly ground pepper

2 egg whites, beaten to soft peaks
4 c. fat-free herb-flavored croutons,
    crushed or processed into 2 c. fine
    crouton crumbs (see note)
2 tbsp. canola oil
Canola cooking spray

1. Preheat the oven to 450° F (230° C). Cut the onions into 1/2-inch-thick slices and separate into rings; reserve the smallest inner rings for another recipe.
2. In a large, deep bowl, combine the flour, beer, cayenne, seasoning salt, and pepper, and whisk together. Gently fold in the beaten egg whites; the batter should be light and fluffy. Spread the crouton crumbs in a separate shallow bowl.
3. Coat two 9- x 13-inch baking pans with 1 tablespoon canola oil each. Hook an onion ring on your finger and dip it into the batter, shaking off any excess; then dip it into the crouton crumbs and shake off the excess. Place the ring in one of the prepared baking pans. Repeat with the remaining onions and batter, placing the smaller rings inside the large ones to make use of every inch of the pan. (If you run out of room, you can layer them a little.)
4. Bake for about 25–30 minutes, until lightly browned. Serve immediately.
- **NOTE:** One 5-ounce (140 g) bag of Marie Callender's Herb Seasoned Croutons (fat-free) contains 4 cups of croutons, which is processed into 2 cups of crouton crumbs—exactly the amount you need for this recipe.

NUTRITIONAL ANALYSES (PER SERVING)

	BEFORE	AFTER		BEFORE	AFTER
CALORIES	310	197	CHOLESTEROL	0 MG	0 MG
PROTEIN	4 G	6 G	FIBER	3 G	2 G
CARBOHYDRATE	41 G	30 G	SODIUM	810 MG	230 MG
FAT	14 G	4.5 G	% CALORIES FROM FAT	41	21
SATURATED FAT	2 G	0.3 G	OMEGA-3 FATTY ACIDS	N/A	0.3 G
MONOUNSATURATED FAT	N/A	2.1 G	OMEGA-6 FATTY ACIDS	N/A	0.7 G
POLYUNSATURATED FAT	N/A	1.1 G			

Hurry It Up Hash Browns

MAKES 4 SERVINGS

Eating restaurant hash browns can add up to mucho calories and fat grams. Unfortunately, a quick label check often reveals just as much fat hiding in some of the frozen hash brown patties available at the supermarket. But you can make your own crispy hash browns at home by starting off with no-fat frozen shredded potatoes (Ore-Ida makes a couple of different types) and pan-frying them in a bit of canola oil. Or, if you like, you can eliminate the oil entirely by coating a nonstick skillet with canola cooking spray . . . but I personally prefer making these with a little bit of oil instead of none at all.

1 1/2 tbsp. canola oil

5 c. (about half a 30-oz., or 725 g, bag) frozen country-style shredded hash browns (do not use patties, and be sure no fat or oils were used in processing)

Canola cooking spray

Salt and pepper to taste

1. Place a large, nonstick skillet over medium-high heat. Add the canola oil and tilt the pan to coat.
2. Spread the hash browns evenly into the pan and coat the tops lightly with canola cooking spray. Cover the skillet and cook for about 4 minutes, until the bottom is nicely browned.
3. Flip the hash browns with a large spatula and sprinkle salt and pepper to taste over the top. Cook the other side, uncovered, until browned, about 4 minutes. Enjoy!

NUTRITIONAL ANALYSES (PER SERVING)

	BEFORE	AFTER		BEFORE	AFTER
CALORIES	260	145	CHOLESTEROL	0 MG	0 MG
PROTEIN	2 G	2 G	FIBER	2 G	2 G
CARBOHYDRATE	28 G	23 G	SODIUM	660 MG	5 MG
FAT	16 G	5.5 G	% CALORIES FROM FAT	55	34
SATURATED FAT	3 G	0.4 G	OMEGA-3 FATTY ACIDS	N/A	0.5 G
MONOUNSATURATED FAT	N/A	3.1 G	OMEGA-6 FATTY ACIDS	N/A	1.1 G
POLYUNSATURATED FAT	N/A	1.6 G			

Skillet Potatoes

MAKES 6 SERVINGS

By using boiled potatoes in this recipe, you don't have to worry about frying the potatoes until they're cooked but can instead concentrate on giving them a nice golden crust. It also means less time in the frying pan, which means less fat as well! These are delicious served alongside your favorite egg dish with a generous dollop of ketchup.

6 large potatoes, boiled and cooled (leave skins on)
2 tbsp. canola oil
1 c. chopped onion
1 green pepper, stemmed, seeded, and chopped

1/2 tsp. salt
1/4 tsp. white pepper
1/2 tsp. dried thyme leaves

1. Cut the potatoes into 1/2-inch dice.
2. Heat a nonstick electric skillet to 400° F (200° C), or place a large nonstick skillet over medium-high heat. Add the canola oil and spread evenly with a spatula. Add the potatoes, onion, and green pepper. Cook for about 3–4 minutes until brown on the bottom, then flip with the spatula to brown the other side—about 3–4 minutes more.
3. Sprinkle the salt, pepper, and thyme over the top and stir. Cook for another 2–4 minutes or until the potatoes are golden brown. Serve immediately.

NUTRITIONAL ANALYSES (PER SERVING)

	BEFORE	AFTER		BEFORE	AFTER
CALORIES	278	200	CHOLESTEROL	5 MG	0 MG
PROTEIN	5 G	4 G	FIBER	4 G	4 G
CARBOHYDRATE	28 G	37 G	SODIUM	744 MG	202 MG
FAT	13 G	5 G	% CALORIES FROM FAT	42	22
SATURATED FAT	4 G	0.4 G	OMEGA-3 FATTY ACIDS	N/A	0.5 G
MONOUNSATURATED FAT	N/A	2.8 G	OMEGA-6 FATTY ACIDS	N/A	1 G
POLYUNSATURATED FAT	N/A	1.5 G			

Seasoned Oven Fries

MAKES 4 SERVINGS

Most people never get tired of eating french fries, so I've included a few french fry recipes in this book. These taste great on their own, but if you're craving a more substantial snack, you can try the Restaurant Cheese Fries on the next page.

4 medium-sized russet potatoes, peeled
2 tbsp. canola oil
1 1/4 tsp. salt
1 1/4 tsp. garlic powder

1 tsp. ground black pepper
3/4-tsp. onion powder
  (or 1 tsp. onion-and-herb seasoning)
1/4-tsp. dried thyme leaves

1. Preheat oven to 450º F (230º C). Cut the potatoes into 1/3-inch wide french fries (they will be as long as the potatoes). Soak the potatoes in a large bowl filled with ice water for about 30 minutes.
2. Coat a nonstick jellyroll pan (10- x 15-inch) with the canola oil, using a pastry brush.
3. Place the remaining ingredients in a small bowl and stir to blend well; set aside.
4. Remove the french fries from the water and blot them dry with a clean kitchen towel.
5. Spread the french fries evenly in the prepared pan, tossing them with your hands to coat well with canola oil. Place in oven and bake until golden (about 20–30 minutes).
6. Remove from the oven and while hot sprinkle with a teaspoon or two of the seasoning mixture; toss to coat well. (Add more seasoning mixture to taste.) Serve immediately.

NUTRITIONAL ANALYSES (PER SERVING)

	BEFORE	AFTER		BEFORE	AFTER
CALORIES	339	206	CHOLESTEROL	0 MG	0 MG
PROTEIN	5 G	3 G	FIBER	3 G	2.5 G
CARBOHYDRATE	50 G	34 G	SODIUM	900 MG	395 MG
FAT	20 G	7 G	% CALORIES FROM FAT	53	30
SATURATED FAT	5 G	0.5 G	OMEGA-3 FATTY ACIDS	N/A	0.7 G
MONOUNSATURATED FAT	N/A	4.1 G	OMEGA-6 FATTY ACIDS	N/A	1.5 G
POLYUNSATURATED FAT	N/A	2.2 G			

Restaurant Cheese Fries

MAKES 4 SERVINGS

2/3 c. shredded reduced fat Monterey Jack or mozzarella cheese

2/3 c. shredded reduced fat cheddar cheese

1 recipe of Seasoned Oven Fries (opposite page)

2-3 slices of turkey bacon, cooked until crisp, crumbled

Combine the cheeses in a medium bowl. Remove the Seasoned Oven Fries from the oven, leaving them in the pan, and sprinkle the cheese evenly over the fries. Top with the bacon and return to the oven for a few minutes, until cheese is melted. Serve hot with Quick Ranch Dip (see page 51) or your favorite barbecue sauce.

NUTRITIONAL ANALYSES (PER SERVING, NOT INCLUDING SAUCE)

	BEFORE	AFTER		BEFORE	AFTER
CALORIES	686	336	CHOLESTEROL	76	34 MG
PROTEIN	23	14 G	FIBER	4 G	2.5 G
CARBOHYDRATES	45	35 G	SODIUM	900 MG	838 MG
FAT	45	16 G	% CALORIES FROM FAT	59	43
SATURATED FAT	19	6.4 G	OMEGA-3 FATTY ACIDS	0 G	0.7 G
MONOUNSATURATED FAT	9.8	4.8 G	OMEGA-6 FATTY ACIDS	1.4	1.9 G
POLYUNSATURATED FAT	1.6	2.6 G			

Crispy Fish Fillet Sandwich
with **Two Tartar Sauces**

MAKES 4 SANDWICHES

Although the fish sandwiches at fast-food restaurants might seem like a healthy option, they're usually deep-fried in vats of oil. For this sandwich, we cut the fat and calories by pan-frying the fillets in canola oil, then give them a lovely texture by coating them in cracker crumbs. Although the fillets are wonderful "naked," I like to turn them into a lighter version of the fast-food sandwich by serving them on hamburger buns with a slice of low-fat cheddar, some lettuce, and a small dollop of homemade tartar sauce.

3/4 lb. skinless, boneless grouper or
   snapper fillets
3/4 c. unbleached or all-purpose flour
1/2 c. low-fat buttermilk
3/4 c. stoned wheat cracker crumbs
   (see note)
1/2 tsp. salt
1/2 tsp. pepper
1/4 tsp. garlic powder

1 tbsp. finely chopped fresh parsley
1 tbsp. canola oil
Canola cooking spray
4 thin slices reduced-fat cheddar cheese
   (about 3 oz., or 85 g)
4 whole-grain hamburger buns
4 large lettuce leaves, rinsed and patted dry
Zesty Tartar Sauce or Fast & Light Tartar
   Sauce, for serving (recipes follow)

1. Cut the fish fillets into four roughly even pieces about 3 1/2 x 3 1/2 inches. Rinse the fish and dry well.
2. Place the flour in a small bowl, and the buttermilk in another small bowl. In a medium, shallow bowl, stir together the wheat cracker crumbs, salt, pepper, garlic powder, and fresh parsley to blend well.
3. Dip each fish square into the flour first, then the buttermilk, then the cracker crumb mixture.
4. Place a medium, nonstick frying pan over medium-high heat. Spread the canola oil on the

NUTRITIONAL ANALYSES (PER SERVING, INCLUDING TARTAR SAUCE)

	BEFORE	AFTER		BEFORE	AFTER
CALORIES	700	340	CHOLESTEROL	90 MG	47 MG
PROTEIN	26 G	29 G	FIBER	3 G	3 G
CARBOHYDRATE	56 G	34 G	SODIUM	980 MG	637 MG
FAT	41 G	9.5 G	% CALORIES FROM FAT	53	26
SATURATED FAT	6 G	4 G	OMEGA-3 FATTY ACIDS	N/A	1.0 G
MONOUNSATURATED FAT	N/A	2.2 G	OMEGA-6 FATTY ACIDS	N/A	0.7 G
POLYUNSATURATED FAT	N/A	2 G			

bottom and add the fillets. Use canola cooking spray to generously coat the tops of the fish. Fry the fillets until the bottoms are golden brown, about 3 minutes, then carefully flip with a spatula and brown the other side—about 2 minutes more. Turn off the heat, lay the cheese slices over the fish, and cover the pan until the cheese melts, about 1 minute.

5. Remove the fillets from the pan and serve on toasted hamburger buns dressed with lettuce and tartar sauce.

• **NOTE:** To make cracker crumbs, place crackers in a zip-top bag and crush with a rolling pin or heavy can.

Zesty Tartar Sauce

MAKES ABOUT 1 1/4 C

1/2 c. light or low-fat mayonnaise
1/2 c. fat-free or light sour cream
1/4 c. finely chopped dill pickle
3 tbsp. finely chopped green onions
1 tbsp. drained and finely chopped
   capers (optional)
1 tbsp. finely chopped fresh parsley
   (or 1 1/2 tsp. dried parsley)

1 tsp. Dijon mustard (regular prepared mustard can be substituted)
1/2 tsp. dried tarragon
1/2 tsp. Worcestershire sauce
1/4 tsp. hot pepper sauce
1/4 tsp. salt
Ground black pepper, to taste

Whisk all the ingredients together in a small bowl. Add pepper to taste. Serve immediately or cover and store in refrigerator for 3 to 5 days.

NUTRITIONAL ANALYSES (PER TBSP.)

	BEFORE	AFTER		BEFORE	AFTER
CALORIES	48	27	CHOLESTEROL	5 MG	3 MG
PROTEIN	0 G	0.4 G	FIBER	0 G	0.1 G
CARBOHYDRATE	2 G	2 G	SODIUM	130 MG	125 MG
FAT	5 G	2 G	% CALORIES FROM FAT	94	66
SATURATED FAT	1 G	0.4 G	OMEGA-3 FATTY ACIDS	N/A	0 G
MONOUNSATURATED FAT	N/A	0.4 G	OMEGA-6 FATTY ACIDS	N/A	0.8 G
POLYUNSATURATED FAT	N/A	1 G			

Fast & Light Tartar Sauce

MAKES ABOUT 10 TBSP.

1/4 c. light mayonnaise
1/4 c. fat-free or light sour cream
1 tbsp. sweet pickle relish

1 tbsp. finely chopped onion
1 tbsp. finely chopped fresh parsley
Ground black pepper, to taste

Whisk all the ingredients together in a small bowl. Add pepper to taste. Serve immediately or cover and store in refrigerator for 3 to 5 days.

NUTRITIONAL ANALYSES (PER TBSP.)

	BEFORE	AFTER		BEFORE	AFTER
CALORIES	48	28	CHOLESTEROL	5 MG	3 MG
PROTEIN	0 G	0.4 G	FIBER	0 G	0.1 G
CARBOHYDRATE	2 G	2 G	SODIUM	130 MG	69 MG
FAT	5 G	2 G	CALORIES FROM FAT	94	66
SATURATED FAT	1 G	0.4 G	OMEGA-3 FATTY ACIDS	N/A	0 G
MONOUNSATURATED FAT	N/A	0.4 G	OMEGA-6 FATTY ACIDS	N/A	0.8 G
POLYUNSATURATED FAT	N/A	1 G			

Santa Fe Chicken Nachos

MAKES 4 SERVINGS

These chicken nachos are layered with different flavors and textures—crunchy homemade tortilla chips, tender chicken, creamy cheese, earthy green onions, spicy salsa, and cool sour cream. Good for you and filling, a plate of these really hits the spot.

2 tsp. canola oil
2 tsp. minced garlic
6 green onions, white parts and green parts sliced separately
2 roasted boneless, skinless chicken breast halves, shredded (about 2 packed c. shredded chicken)
1 c. salsa (1/2 c. taco sauce can be substituted*)

2 recipes Oven-Baked Tortilla Chips (see page 124)
1 1/4–1 1/2 c. (5–6 oz., or 140–170 g) shredded reduced-fat cheddar and Monterey Jack cheese blend
2 large tomatoes, diced
1 c. fat-free sour cream, for garnish (optional)

1. Preheat the broiler.
2. Place the canola oil in a medium nonstick saucepan over medium heat. Add the garlic and the whites of the green onions to the oil and sauté for about 1 minute. Stir in the shredded chicken and sauté for 1 minute more. Stir in the salsa and remove from the heat.
3. Heap the tortilla chips onto a jelly roll pan, spoon the chicken mixture evenly over the top, then sprinkle with the cheese and tomatoes. Place under the broiler until the cheese melts, 1–2 minutes. Remove from the broiler and sprinkle with the remaining green onions. Add a dollop of fat-free sour cream and serve in the pan or divide among four plates.

NUTRITIONAL ANALYSES (PER SERVING)

	BEFORE	AFTER		BEFORE	AFTER
CALORIES	770	428	CHOLESTEROL	69 MG	35 MG
PROTEIN	21 G	30 G	FIBER	5 G	5 G
CARBOHYDRATE	84 G	43 G	SODIUM	1310 MG	175 MG
FAT	39 G	15.5 G	% CALORIES FROM FAT	46	32
SATURATED FAT	11 G	7 G	OMEGA-3 FATTY ACIDS	N/A	0.5 G
MONOUNSATURATED FAT	N/A	3.7 G	OMEGA-6 FATTY ACIDS	N/A	2 G
POLYUNSATURATED FAT	N/A	2.5 G	*Nutritional analyses do not account for substitutions.		

Oven-Baked Tortilla Chips

MAKES 2 SERVINGS

My kids actually like these better than the fried kind! Imagine that. The trick is baking the chips until they're crispy but removing them from the oven before they get too brown. These are perfect for Santa Fe Chicken Nachos (page 123) and Beef and Bean Nachos Grande (page 129), but they're also irresistible on their own.

4 6-inch corn tortillas
Canola cooking spray

1 tsp. canola oil
Salt or seasoning salt, to taste

1. Preheat the oven to 375° F (190° C). Cut each tortilla into eight wedges.
2. Coat a nonstick jelly roll (or similar) pan with canola cooking spray. Lay the tortilla wedges along the entire bottom of the prepared pan. (The tortillas can overlap, but only slightly.)
3. Brush the tops of the wedges lightly with canola oil. Sprinkle salt or seasoning salt over the top if desired.
4. Place the chips in the oven and bake until crispy but not too brown; check them after 15 minutes. If they're not yet crispy, bake for 2 minutes more and check again. Repeat the baking and checking at 2-minute intervals until the tortilla chips are crisp and light golden brown.

NUTRITIONAL ANALYSES (PER APPROXIMATELY 2-OZ., OR 60 G, SERVING)

	BEFORE	AFTER		BEFORE	AFTER
CALORIES	284	136	CHOLESTEROL	0 MG	0 MG
PROTEIN	4 G	3 G	FIBER	3 G	3 G
CARBOHYDRATE	35 G	24 G	SODIUM	300 MG	83 MG
FAT	14 G	3.6 G	% CALORIES FROM FAT	44	24
SATURATED FAT	3 G	0.3 G	OMEGA-3 FATTY ACIDS	0.1 G	0.3 G
MONOUNSATURATED FAT	8.7 G	1.7 G	OMEGA-6 FATTY ACIDS	1.9 G	1 G
POLYUNSATURATED FAT	2 G	1.3 G			

Spicy Chicken Fingers

MAKES 4 SERVINGS

These are great in a sandwich (see page 128) or on their own, with ketchup, honey mustard, or barbecue sauce. Be sure to brown the crust well before baking.

Canola cooking spray
4 boneless, skinless chicken breasts, each
    cut into 4 lengthwise strips (or 1 lb.,
    454 g, chicken tenders)
1 c. unbleached white flour
1 c. mashed potato flakes (such as Idaho Spuds)
3–6 tsp. Creole or Cajun seasoning
1 1/2 tsp. salt

1 tsp. ground black pepper
2 tsp. ground oregano
1 tsp. garlic powder
3/4 c. fat-free half-and-half (low-fat or
    whole milk can be substituted*)
1 egg
1 tbsp. canola oil

1. Preheat the oven to 450° F (230° C). Line a 9- x 9-inch baking dish with foil, and coat the foil with canola cooking spray.
2. Rinse the chicken breasts, then pat them dry with paper towels; set aside.
3. Place the flour, potato flakes, Cajun spice blend, salt, pepper, oregano, and garlic powder in a small bowl, and stir to blend well.
4. In another small bowl, combine the half-and-half and egg; beat with a fork until smooth.
5. Place a large, heavy skillet over medium-high heat. Add the canola oil and spread evenly over the bottom of the pan. Proceed immediately to the next step.
6. Dip each chicken strip first in the flour mixture, then in the egg mixture, then back in the flour mixture and place in the hot pan. Repeat with the remaining chicken strips. Spray the tops with canola cooking spray.
7. When the bottoms of strips are nicely browned, about 3–4 minutes, flip and brown the other side about 3–4 minutes more. Remove the chicken strips to the prepared baking dish.
8. Place the chicken in the oven to finish cooking—about 15 minutes, or until the thickest part of the breast is cooked through.

NUTRITIONAL ANALYSES (PER SERVING)

	BEFORE	AFTER		BEFORE	AFTER
CALORIES	473	272	CHOLESTEROL	99 MG	90 MG
PROTEIN	33 G	32 G	FIBER	1 G	1 G
CARBOHYDRATE	31 G	18 G	SODIUM	1520 MG	540 MG
FAT	20 G	7 G	% CALORIES FROM FAT	38	26
SATURATED FAT	5.5 G	1.4 G	OMEGA-3 FATTY ACIDS	N/A	0.4 G
MONOUNSATURATED FAT	N/A	3.4 G	OMEGA-6 FATTY ACIDS	N/A	1.4 G
POLYUNSATURATED FAT	N/A	1.8 G	*Nutritional analyses do not account for substitutions.		

All-White-Meat Easy Chicken Nuggets

MAKES ABOUT 22 NUGGETS (5 SERVINGS)

For the longest time, one of my daughters would only eat chicken nuggets from Wendy's—until now. These oven-fried all-white-meat nuggets passed even her inspection. You can double the recipe and freeze some in zip-top freezer bags for a quick snack or entrée later in the week (simply reheat them in a toaster oven).

1 tbsp. canola oil

1 1/4 lb. (565 g) chicken tenders, skinless, tendons removed (or 1 1/4 lb. (565 g.) ground white meat chicken or turkey)

1 egg white

2 tbsp. low-fat buttermilk

1 tbsp. Wondra quick-mixing flour

1 c. unbleached or all-purpose flour

2 tsp. freshly cracked black pepper

2 tsp. salt

1/4 tsp. ground cayenne pepper

Canola cooking spray

1. Preheat the oven to 450° F (230° C). Spread 1 tablespoon of canola oil over the bottom of a 9- x 13-inch baking pan; set aside.
2. Place the chicken tenders, egg white, buttermilk, and Wondra flour in a food processor. Pulse until a ground-meat mixture forms—similar in consistency to hamburger but moister—about 8 seconds. (If you do not have a food processor, mix together ground chicken with egg white, buttermilk and Wondra flour in a large bowl.)
3. Place the unbleached flour, black pepper, salt, and cayenne pepper in a small bowl and blend well with a fork or whisk.
4. Scoop out a level tablespoon of the ground chicken mixture to form a nugget and drop it into the small bowl of seasoned flour; coat all sides well. Place the nugget in the prepared pan. Repeat with the remaining ground chicken mixture. Use canola cooking spray to generously coat the top of the chicken nuggets (spray about 10 inches from the surface).
5. Bake in the center of the oven for 15 minutes. Flip the nuggets with a spatula and bake for 10 minutes more. Remove from the oven and serve hot.

NUTRITIONAL ANALYSES (PER SERVING)

	BEFORE	AFTER		BEFORE	AFTER
CALORIES	240	197	CHOLESTEROL	65 MG	50 MG
PROTEIN	11 G	29 G	FIBER	0 G	0.4 G
CARBOHYDRATE	11 G	9 G	SODIUM	549 MG	500 MG
FAT	16 G	4 G	% CALORIES FROM FAT	60	18
SATURATED FAT	3 G	0.6 G	OMEGA-3 FATTY ACIDS	N/A	0.3 G
MONOUNSATURATED FAT	7.2 G	2 G	OMEGA-6 FATTY ACIDS	N/A	0.8 G
POLYUNSATURATED FAT	3.5 G	1.2 G			

Finger-Lickin' Chicken Sandwich

MAKES 4 SANDWICHES

So many of my friends love fast-food chicken sandwiches made with deep-fried breaded chicken patties. To me, these oven-fried breaded chicken breasts taste just as good, and the difference in calories and fat grams is huge.

1 recipe Finger-Lickin' Good Chicken
  (see page 92)
4 slices reduced-fat mild or sharp cheddar
  cheese (about 3/4 oz., or 22 g, per slice)
4 multigrain or whole wheat hamburger
  buns (toasted, if desired)

4 large tomato slices
4 large lettuce leaves
4 tbsp. ketchup (barbecue sauce or mustard can be substituted)

1. Prepare Finger Lickin' Good Chicken according to the recipe, but approximately 5 minutes before the chicken is done, top each piece with a slice of cheese.
2. Serve each cheese-topped chicken breast on a bun with a slice of tomato, lettuce leaf, and ketchup if desired.

NUTRITIONAL ANALYSES (PER SANDWICH)

	BEFORE	AFTER		BEFORE	AFTER
CALORIES	510	422	CHOLESTEROL	89 MG	50 MG
PROTEIN	22 G	40 G	FIBER	3 G	5 G
CARBOHYDRATE	47 G	38 G	SODIUM	1090 MG	880 MG
FAT	26 G	12 G	% CALORIES FROM FAT	46	26
SATURATED FAT	8.5 G	4.7 G	OMEGA-3 FATTY ACIDS	N/A	0.3 G
MONOUNSATURATED FAT	N/A	3.4 G	OMEGA-6 FATTY ACIDS	N/A	1.6 G
POLYUNSATURATED FAT	N/A	2 G			

Triple-Crunch Sandwich

MAKES 5 SANDWICHES

This dish is modeled after the KFC sandwich, which serves three chicken strips on a hamburger bun. This version has a lot fewer calories and less fat because we're baking the chicken—and dressing it with a lighter condiment while we're at it!

5 multigrain hamburger buns
5 tbsp. barbecue sauce, ketchup,
    or mustard
1 recipe Spicy Chicken Fingers
    (see page 125)

5 lettuce leaves
5 onion slices
5 large tomato slices

1. Toast the hamburger buns, if desired. Dress the bottom of each bun with barbecue sauce, ketchup, or mustard.
2. Place three chicken fingers on each bun and top with a lettuce leaf, slice of onion, and tomato.

NUTRITIONAL ANALYSES (PER SANDWICH)

	BEFORE	AFTER		BEFORE	AFTER
CALORIES	550	350	CHOLESTEROL	85 MG	73 MG
PROTEIN	28 G	30 G	FIBER	2 G	3.5 G
CARBOHYDRATE	36 G	38 G	SODIUM	830 MG	750 MG
FAT	32 G	8.5 G	% CALORIES FROM FAT	52	22
SATURATED FAT	7 G	1.7 G	OMEGA-3 FATTY ACIDS	N/A	0.4 G
MONOUNSATURATED FAT	N/A	4 G	OMEGA-6 FATTY ACIDS	N/A	1.7 G
POLYUNSATURATED FAT	N/A	2.1 G			

Beef & Bean Nachos Grande

MAKES 4 SERVINGS

The nachos at Taco Bell consist of a mound of deep-fried tortilla chips smothered in beans, seasoned ground beef, cheese sauce, green onions, sour cream, and chopped tomatoes. Certainly tasty, but not good for you. But at home we can make a much lighter version by using lower-fat chips, leaner beef and beans, fat-free or light sour cream, and a little less cheese sauce. Check out the difference in calories and fat grams!

1 pound super lean ground beef (or ground sirloin)

1 ounce packet taco spices and seasonings (e.g. Lawry's)

2/3 c.water

15 ounce can kidney beans, rinsed and drained

8 c.reduced-fat tortilla chips (store bought or homemade, see Oven-Baked Tortilla Chips, page 124)

1/2 c.Nacho Cheese Sauce (use bottled products with 5 grams of fat or less per 2 tbsp.)

1/4 c.chopped green onions, whites and part of greens

1/2 c.chopped tomatoes

1/2 c.fat free sour cream (light sour cream can be substituted*)

1. In large nonstick skillet or frying pan over medium-high heat, brown beef and break up with a wooden spoon until crumbly. Add taco seasoning packet, water, and beans and mix thoroughly. Bring to a boil; reduce heat to low and cook, uncovered, about 6 minutes, stirring occasionally. Remove from heat and cover to keep warm.
2. Spread chips out on 4 dinner plates and distribute beef-and-bean mixture on top.
3. Place nacho cheese sauce in saucepan over low heat until warm (or microwave on high for 1–2 minutes); pour over nachos.
4. Top with green onions, chopped tomatoes, and sour cream and serve.

NUTRITIONAL ANALYSES (PER SERVING)

	BEFORE	AFTER		BEFORE	AFTER
CALORIES	633	435	CHOLESTEROL	49 MG	40 MG
PROTEIN	22 G	23 G	FIBER	7G	7 G
CARBOHYDRATE	60 G	65 G	SODIUM	952 MG	770 MG
FAT	34 G	10 G	% CALORIES FROM FAT	48	21
SATURATED FAT	12.3 G	3.4 G	OMEGA-3 FATTY ACIDS	N/A	0.8 G
MONOUNSATURATED FAT	N/A	3.2 G	OMEGA-6 FATTY ACIDS	N/A	1.6 G
POLYUNSATURATED FAT	N/A	3 G	*Nutritional analyses do not account for substitutions.		

Baked Mini Corn Dogs

MAKES ABOUT 5 SERVINGS (4 MINI CORN DOGS PER SERVING)

Grab your favorite light hot dogs, mix yourself up a batch of this corn dog batter, and light mini corn dogs are only 15 minutes away! You can even make some extras and keep them in the freezer for a last-minute snack; just warm them up in the microwave.

Canola cooking spray
1/2 c. yellow cornmeal
1/2 c. unbleached white flour
1 tbsp. sugar
1 tsp. dry mustard
1 tsp. baking powder

1/2 tsp. salt
1/2 c. low-fat or whole milk
1/4 c. egg substitute (such as
    Egg Beaters) or 1 large egg, beaten*
1 tbsp. canola oil
4 light hot dogs (please avoid "plump" type)

1. Preheat the oven to 375° F (190° C). Generously coat the insides of about 20 nonstick mini muffin cups with canola cooking spray.
2. Combine the cornmeal, flour, sugar, mustard, baking powder and salt in a large mixing bowl and stir together. Add the milk, egg substitute, and canola oil and beat with an electric mixer on medium-low speed until smooth.
3. Cut the hot dogs into approximately 1-inch lengths (laid on its side, each piece should fit nicely into a mini muffin cup).
4. Place each hot dog piece on its side in a mini muffin cup. Spoon about 1 tablespoon of batter on top of each piece.
5. Place the muffin pan in the oven and bake for about 15 minutes or until cooked through (it will look like a mini corn muffin with a hot dog in the center).

NUTRITIONAL ANALYSES (PER SERVING)

	BEFORE	AFTER		BEFORE	AFTER
CALORIES	290	200	CHOLESTEROL	44 MG	14 MG
PROTEIN	8 G	10 G	FIBER	0 G	1.5 G
CARBOHYDRATE	23 G	28 G	SODIUM	750 MG	670 MG
FAT	18 G	5.5 G	% CALORIES FROM FAT	56	25
SATURATED FAT	5 G	1.3 G	OMEGA-3 FATTY ACIDS	N/A	0.3 G
MONOUNSATURATED FAT	N/A	2 G	OMEGA-6 FATTY ACIDS	N/A	0.7 G
POLYUNSATURATED FAT	N/A	1 G	*Nutritional analyses do not account for substitutions.		

Double-Decker Taco

MAKES 8 TACOS (ABOUT 4 SERVINGS)

One of these homemade tacos contains half the fat of a Double Decker Taco Supreme from Taco Bell.

1 lb. (454 g) superlean ground beef (such as ground sirloin)
1/4 c. all-purpose flour
1 tbsp. chili powder
1 tsp. salt
1/3 c. finely minced yellow or white onion
1/4 tsp. garlic powder
1/2 c. water
Canola cooking spray

1 16-oz. (454 g) can fat-free refried beans
8 (6-inch-diameter) flour tortillas
1 c. shredded reduced-fat cheddar cheese, divided
8 crispy corn taco shells (store-bought or light homemade; see page 104)
2 c. finely shredded iceberg lettuce
Taco sauce (Ortega and Taco Bell brands are available in bottles), optional

1. In a large mixing bowl, combine the ground beef, flour, chili powder, salt, onion, garlic powder, and water. Beat with an electric mixer on its lowest speed until well blended.
2. Place a large nonstick frying pan over medium-high heat. Coat the pan with canola cooking spray and add the beef mixture. Cook the mixture until brown, breaking up the meat into small pieces with a spatula while it cooks, about 6 minutes. The filling should end up being somewhat thick without large chunks of beef.
3. While the beef is cooking, warm the refried beans in a small saucepan over medium-low heat.
4. When the beans and beef are ready, spread 1/8 cup of hot refried beans over the top of a flour tortilla and sprinkle with a tablespoon of the grated cheese. Wrap the prepared flour tortilla around a crispy corn taco shell and spoon 1/8 cup of the beef mixture inside the corn tortilla. Sprinkle with a tablespoon or two of grated cheese and 1/4 cup of the shredded lettuce. Drizzle with taco sauce if desired. Repeat to assemble the remaining double-decker tacos.

NUTRITIONAL ANALYSES (PER TACO)

	BEFORE	AFTER		BEFORE	AFTER
CALORIES	380	337	CHOLESTEROL	40 MG	40 MG
PROTEIN	15 G	23 G	FIBER	7 G	6 G
CARBOHYDRATE	40 G	43 G	SODIUM	820 MG	840 MG
FAT	18 G	8 G	% CALORIES FROM FAT	N/A	21
SATURATED FAT	8 G	3.7 G	OMEGA-3 FATTY ACIDS	N/A	0.3 G
MONOUNSATURATED FAT	N/A	2.4 G	OMEGA-6 FATTY ACIDS	N/A	0.6 G
POLYUNSATURATED FAT	N/A	0.9 G			

French Toast Sticks with Creamy Vanilla Dip & Cinnamon Pancake Syrup

MAKES 4 SERVINGS (4 LARGE FRENCH TOAST STICKS PER SERVING)

A serving of five small French toast sticks from Burger King gives you 630 calories and 30 grams of fat, which makes you wonder whether they're deep-fried. Just in case they are, here's a light version. We're using sandwich rolls (French or sourdough) and cutting off the crusts to make perfectly sized, firmer-textured French toast sticks. These are really nice paired with Creamy Vanilla Dip or Cinnamon Pancake Syrup (recipes follow) and some fresh fruit.

2 large eggs
    (high-omega-3 eggs if available)
1/2 c. egg substitute
    (such as Egg Beaters)
1 c. low-fat buttermilk
1/4 tsp. ground cinnamon
Pinch of ground nutmeg

Pinch of salt
1/4 c. granulated sugar
4 long French or sourdough sandwich
    rolls (about 2 3/4 oz., or 71 g, each),
    not precut
4 tsp. canola oil
Canola cooking spray

1. Place the eggs, egg substitute, buttermilk, cinnamon, nutmeg, salt, and sugar in a mixing bowl and beat or whisk together until thoroughly combined.
2. Carefully cut off all the crusts of each sandwich roll (bottom, top, and sides) to make a rectangle. Then cut each roll lengthwise into four sticks, about 5 x 2 x 3/4 inch each.
3. Place a medium nonstick frying pan over medium heat and coat the bottom with 2 teaspoons of canola oil. Add the bread sticks, five or six at a time, to the bowl with the egg and let them soak until moist in the center, about 10 seconds. Place about eight sticks (or as many as you can fit in a single layer) in the pan, coat the tops with canola cooking spray, and cook until the bottom is golden brown, about 2 minutes. Flip the sticks over

NUTRITIONAL ANALYSES (PER SERVING, WITHOUT DIP OR SYRUP)

	BEFORE	AFTER		BEFORE	AFTER
CALORIES	630	421	CHOLESTEROL	82 MG	7.5 MG
PROTEIN	11 G	14 G	FIBER	3 G	3 G
CARBOHYDRATE	75 G	63 G	SODIUM	800 MG	660 MG
FAT	30 G	12 G	CALORIES FROM FAT	43	25
SATURATED FAT	6 G	2.4 G	OMEGA-3 FATTY ACIDS	N/A	0.5 G
MONOUNSATURATED FAT	N/A	6.1 G	OMEGA-6 FATTY ACIDS	N/A	2.1 G
POLYUNSATURATED FAT	N/A	2.6 G			

and cook until the second side is golden brown, about 2 minutes more. Repeat with the remaining bread sticks and canola oil.

4. Serve hot with Creamy Vanilla Dip or Reduced-Fat Pancake Syrup and fresh fruit.

Creamy Vanilla Dip

MAKES ABOUT 6 TBSP.

6 tbsp. powdered sugar
2 tbsp. light cream cheese

3 tsp. fat-free half-and-half (more if needed for desired consistency)
1/2 tsp. vanilla extract

Place all the ingredients in a small mixing bowl or small food processor and mix until well blended. Add more half-and-half as needed (the consistency should be creamy but not too thick). Serve immediately.

FRY LIGHT, FRY RIGHT PREPARATION (PER TBSP)*

CALORIES	38	FIBER	0 G
PROTEIN	1 G	SODIUM	20 MG
CARBOHYDRATE	8 G	% CALORIES FROM FAT	9
FAT	0.4 G	OMEGA-3 FATTY ACIDS	0 G
SATURATED FAT	0.3 G	OMEGA-6 FATTY ACIDS	0 G
MONOUNSATURATED FAT	0 G		
POLYUNSATURATED FAT	0 G	*Original recipe not based on traditional.	
CHOLESTEROL	2 MG		

Cinnamon Pancake Syrup

MAKES ABOUT 2 1/3 C.

1 c. water
3 c. dark brown sugar, packed

1/2 tsp. ground cinnamon
2 tsp. vanilla extract

Place the water in a medium nonstick saucepan and bring to a boil over medium-high heat. Once it comes to a boil, reduce the heat to medium-low and stir in the brown sugar and cinnamon. Stir constantly with wooden spoon until the sugar is completely dissolved, about 5 minutes. Stir in the vanilla and remove the syrup from the heat. Pour the syrup into a jar and serve, or store in refrigerator for up to 2 weeks.

FRY LIGHT, FRY RIGHT PREPARATION (PER TBSP)*

CALORIES	67	FIBER	0 G
PROTEIN	0 G	SODIUM	7 MG
CARBOHYDRATE	17 G	% CALORIES FROM FAT	0
FAT	0 G	OMEGA-3 FATTY ACIDS	0 G
SATURATED FAT	N/A	OMEGA-6 FATTY ACIDS	0 G
MONOUNSATURATED FAT	N/A		
POLYUNSATURATED FAT	N/A	*Nutritional analysis does not differ significantly	
CHOLESTEROL	0 MG	from traditional preparation.	

Better-Than-Domino's Dots

MAKES ABOUT 6 SERVINGS (4 "DOTS" PER SERVING)

These are a light take on the cinnamon-sugar Dots that Domino's Pizza makes.
They are just as fun to make as they are to eat—a family favorite! These are great
served with the Creamy Vanilla Dip on page 133.

Canola cooking spray
1 1-lb. (454 g) loaf frozen bread dough
   (such as Bridgford Ready-Dough),
   thawed

1 1/2 tbsp. butter
1/2 c. granulated sugar
2 tsp. ground cinnamon

1. Cover a jelly roll pan with foil and coat the foil with canola cooking spray.
2. Cut the thawed bread dough into 24 equal pieces. (You can cut the loaf into eight slices
   then cut each slice into three pieces.) Roll each piece into a ball.
3. Place the butter in a microwave-safe custard cup and cook on high for 30 seconds or until
   the butter has melted. (Or place the butter in a small saucepan over low heat until melted;
   remove from the heat.) Meanwhile, combine the sugar and cinnamon in a small bowl and
   blend well with a spoon.
4. Roll each bread ball into the melted butter to coat, then coat with the cinnamon-sugar
   mixture. Place each bread ball on the prepared jelly roll pan, making sure they do
   not touch.
5. Place the jelly roll pan in a warm place in your kitchen and let the dough rise until almost
   double in size, about 45 minutes. Halfway through, preheat the oven to 375° F (190° C).
6. Place the jelly roll pan in the oven and bake the "dots" until they're cooked through,
   about 18–20 minutes. Serve warm.

NUTRITIONAL ANALYSES (PER SERVING)

	BEFORE	AFTER		BEFORE	AFTER
CALORIES	360	299	CHOLESTEROL	0 MG	8 MG
PROTEIN	4.5 G	8 G	FIBER	1.5 G	1.5 G
CARBOHYDRATE	42 G	55 G	SODIUM	435 MG	450 MG
FAT	19 G	6 G	% CALORIES FROM FAT	48	18
SATURATED FAT	3.8 G	1.8 G	OMEGA-3 FATTY ACIDS	N/A	0.04 G
MONOUNSATURATED FAT	N/A	0.8 G	OMEGA-6 FATTY ACIDS	N/A	0.06 G
POLYUNSATURATED FAT	N/A	0.1 G			

CHAPTER 7

Almost Sinless Sides

Light Fried Green Tomatoes

MAKES 4 SERVINGS (ABOUT 4–5 SLICES PER SERVING)

This Southern specialty features a great combination of flavors and textures, but usually involves frying the tomatoes in at least 1/2 inch of oil. To create our lighter version, we dip the tomato slices in flour, then eggs, followed by a bread-crumb mixture. This may seem like too much trouble, but it produces a tasty crumb coating that stays on the tomatoes instead of falling off in the pan.

4 large green tomatoes (if you can't find green tomatoes, you can use firm, not-quite-ripe red tomatoes)
1 large egg
1/4 c. egg substitute (such as Egg Beaters)
1/2 c. fat-free half-and-half (low-fat or whole milk can be substituted*)

1 c. unbleached white flour
1/2 c. cornmeal
1/2 c. plain breadcrumbs
1 tsp. coarse kosher salt
1/4 tsp. ground black pepper
1 tbsp. canola oil, divided
Canola cooking spray

1. Slice the tomatoes 1/3 inch thick. Discard the ends.
2. In a medium-sized bowl, whisk together the egg, egg substitute, and fat-free half-and-half. Place the flour in a shallow bowl. Combine the cornmeal, breadcrumbs, salt, and pepper in another shallow bowl. Dip the tomato slices into flour and coat well. Then dip the tomato slices into the egg mixture and dredge in the breadcrumb mixture to completely coat.
3. Place a large nonstick skillet over medium heat and coat the bottom evenly with 1 1/2 teaspoons of canola oil. Place half of the tomatoes into the frying pan (making sure the slices don't touch each other) and coat the tops with canola cooking spray. When the undersides of the tomato slices are browned—about 3–4 minutes—flip and cook the other side until browned, about 3 minutes more. Remove to a plate with paper towels.
4. Repeat with remaining 1 1/2 teaspoons oil and tomato slices.

NUTRITIONAL ANALYSES (PER SERVING)

	BEFORE	AFTER		BEFORE	AFTER
CALORIES	285	226	CHOLESTEROL	41 MG	26 MG
PROTEIN	5 G	8 G	FIBER	1.5 G	4 G
CARBOHYDRATES	19 G	37 G	SODIUM	430 MG	479 MG
FAT	21.5 G	5 G	% CALORIES FROM FAT	68	20
SATURATED FAT	4.6 G	0.5 G	OMEGA-3 FATTY ACIDS	0.5 G	0.3 G
MONOUNSATURATED FAT	9.4 G	2.4 G	OMEGA-6 FATTY ACIDS	5.9 G	1 G
POLYUNSATURATED FAT	6.4 G	1.4 G	*Nutritional analyses do not account for substitutions.		

Oven-Fried Zucchini Sticks

MAKES 8 SERVINGS (4 ZUCCHINI STICKS PER SERVING)

These popular veggie sticks are crunchy on the outside and soft on the inside.
Serve with Quick Ranch Dip (page 51) or Homemade Zesty Pizza Sauce (page 53).

4 medium-sized zucchini
Canola cooking spray
1 tsp. minced or chopped garlic
1/3 c. egg substitute
   (such as Egg Beaters)

1 tbsp. light mayonnaise (regular
   mayonnaise can be substituted*)
1 c. Italian-style breadcrumbs

1. Wash and dry the zucchini. Cut in half lengthwise and widthwise. Then cut each of these pieces into 4 sticks; you should have 32 sticks.
2. Preheat the oven to 400° F (200° C). Generously coat cookie sheets or a large nonstick jelly roll pan with canola cooking spray.
3. Place the garlic, egg substitute, and mayonnaise in the food processor and blend well (or use an electric mixer); spoon into a shallow bowl. Place the breadcrumbs in another shallow bowl.
4. Dip the zucchini sticks, one by one, into the egg mixture first and then the breadcrumb mixture to coat well. Place the coated sticks on the prepared cookie sheets or pan.
5. Spray the tops of the zucchini sticks with canola cooking spray. Bake in the center of the oven for 12 minutes until the outside coating is nice and golden.

NUTRITIONAL ANALYSES (PER SERVING)

	BEFORE	AFTER		BEFORE	AFTER
CALORIES	180	56	CHOLESTEROL	1 MG	1 MG
PROTEIN	3 G	3 G	FIBER	1.5 G	1.5 G
CARBOHYDRATES	9 G	9 G	SODIUM	219 MG	219 MG
FAT	14.2 G	1.2 G	% CALORIES FROM FAT	71	19
SATURATED FAT	1.8 G	0.1 G	OMEGA-3 FATTY ACIDS	0.5 G	0.4 G
MONOUNSATURATED FAT	3.4 G	0.1 G	OMEGA-6 FATTY ACIDS	8.3 G	0.4 G
POLYUNSATURATED FAT	9 G	1 G	*Nutritional analyses do not account for substitutions.		

Vegetable Tempura with Ginger Dipping Sauce

MAKES 6 SERVINGS

Tempura is one of my favorite items to order at a Japanese restaurant, but I can't eat too much of it or my stomach screams back at me. This light tempura is the answer to my woes—the taste of tempura but without all the grease. We're making a slightly thicker batter, then coating the battered veggies with a crumb mixture so that they hold up better to oven baking.

1 c. white rice flour (available at natural food stores and some supermarkets—this is essential for the delicate batter that we come to expect with tempura)
1/4 tsp. baking powder
1 c. ice water
1 large egg, beaten
2 c. panko crumbs (available in Asian food markets and some supermarkets)

1 1/2 lb. (685 g) assorted vegetables, cleaned and well dried (1-inch broccoli or cauliflower florets, green beans, baby carrots, asparagus spears, zucchini sticks, mushrooms, 1/8-inch rounds of peeled sweet or white potatoes, thin wedges of squash, etc.)
Canola oil cooking spray
Ginger Dipping Sauce (recipe follows)

1. Preheat the oven to 450° F (230° C).
2. In a medium-sized bowl, whisk together the rice flour and baking powder. Add the ice water and the beaten egg and stir until just combined (be careful not to overmix). Place the panko crumbs in a shallow bowl.
3. Dip the prepared vegetables one at a time into the batter, shaking off the excess. Then dip them in the panko crumbs, lightly pressing the crumbs into the vegetables to coat.
4. Hold each vegetable in one hand and, with the canola cooking spray 6 inches away in the other, lightly spray all around to add a thin coating of canola oil to the outside.
5. Place on a nonstick jelly roll pan and bake in the preheated oven until crispy on the outside, about 25–30 minutes. Serve with Ginger Dipping Sauce.

NUTRITIONAL ANALYSES (PER SERVING, USING BROCCOLI, SWEET POTATO, AND ASPARAGUS)

	BEFORE	AFTER		BEFORE	AFTER
CALORIES	260	240	CHOLESTEROL	102 MG	35 MG
PROTEIN	7 G	7 G	FIBER	2.5 G	4 G
CARBOHYDRATE	23 G	44 G	SODIUM	69 MG	69 MG
FAT	16 G	4 G	% CALORIES FROM FAT	55	15
SATURATED FAT	3.2 G	0.6 G	OMEGA-3 FATTY ACIDS	0.4 G	0.3 G
MONOUNSATURATED FAT	4.8 G	1.8 G	OMEGA-6 FATTY ACIDS	6.4 G	0.7 G
POLYUNSATURATED FAT	6.8 G	1 G			

Ginger Dipping Sauce

MAKES ABOUT 1 C.

This sauce has just the right amount of zip and zing to perfectly complement Veggie Tempura.

1/2 c. lower-sodium soy sauce (regular soy sauce can be substituted*)
1/4 c. sweet or golden sherry (dry sherry can be substituted in a pinch*)

1/4 c. rice vinegar
1 tbsp. dark or light brown sugar
2 tbsp. bottled minced or chopped fresh gingerroot

Place the first four ingredients in a small nonstick saucepan and bring to a boil over medium-high heat. Cook for about 1 minute. Let the sauce cool completely, then stir in the gingerroot. Serve immediately or cover and keep in the refrigerator for 3 to 5 days.

FRY LIGHT, FRY RIGHT PREPARATION (PER TBSP.)**

CALORIES	14	SODIUM	325 MG
PROTEIN	0.5 G	% CALORIES FROM FAT	0
CARBOHYDRATE	2.5 G	OMEGA-3 FATTY ACIDS	0 G
FAT	0 G	OMEGA-6 FATTY ACIDS	0 G
SATURATED FAT	N/A		
MONOUNSATURATED FAT	N/A	*Nutritional analysis does not account for subtitutions.	
POLYUNSATURATED FAT	N/A	**Nutritional analysis does not differ significantly	
CHOLESTEROL	0 MG	from traditional preparation.	
FIBER	0 G		

Oven-Fried Okra

MAKES 6 SERVINGS

This recipe is the light version of a fried okra recipe common in the South. Normally the okra is coated with a seasoned cornmeal mixture and deep-fried in peanut oil. For the light version, we are soaking the okra slices in buttermilk, coating them with the crumb mixture, then oven-frying them with a bit of cooking spray until golden on the outside and tender inside.

1 lb. (454 g) fresh okra
   (about 36 large okras)
2 c. low-fat buttermilk
1 tbsp. canola oil
1/2 c. cornmeal
1/2 c. unbleached white flour

1/2 tsp. salt, or to taste
1/4 tsp. pepper, or to taste
1/8 tsp. ground cayenne pepper,
   or to taste
Canola cooking spray

1. About 30 minutes before you want to oven-fry the okra, trim the stem ends from the pods and slice the pods into 1/2-inch pieces. Place them in a bowl with the low-fat buttermilk. Stir to coat and soak for 30 minutes.
2. Meanwhile, preheat the oven to 400° F (200° C). Evenly brush the bottom of a nonstick 10- x 15-inch jelly roll pan with a tablespoon of canola oil.
3. Place the cornmeal, flour, salt, pepper, and cayenne pepper in a small bowl and stir to blend well.
4. Remove each piece of okra from the buttermilk one at a time and lay in the bowl with the cornmeal mixture. Coat the outside well, then add to the prepared pan, making sure the pieces don't touch each other. Coat the tops generously with canola cooking spray.
5. Bake the okra for about 15 minutes, then flip and bake for about 10 minutes more, until golden crispy on the outside and tender on the inside.

NUTRITIONAL ANALYSES (PER SERVING)

	BEFORE	AFTER		BEFORE	AFTER
CALORIES	255	134	CHOLESTEROL	1 MG	1 MG
PROTEIN	5 G	5 G	FIBER	3 G	3 G
CARBOHYDRATES	23 G	23 G	SODIUM	218 MG	218 MG
FAT	16.6 G	3 G	% CALORIES FROM FAT	59	20
SATURATED FAT	2.1 G	0.4 G	OMEGA-3 FATTY ACIDS	0.3 G	0.2 G
MONOUNSATURATED FAT	4.8 G	1.5 G	OMEGA-6 FATTY ACIDS	8.5 G	0.6 G
POLYUNSATURATED FAT	8.8 G	0.8 G			

Corn Fritters

MAKES ABOUT 8 SERVINGS (2 FRITTERS PER SERVING)

When I developed this recipe it was the first time I had ever come face to face with a corn fritter. I was skeptical, thinking, how good can a corn pancake taste? I ate my words . . . and half the plate of fritters! For this recipe, we use a lighter egg batter and pan-fry the fritters in a bit of oil. Frozen corn works very well here, though you can also use fresh.

2 large eggs, separated
1 c. frozen or fresh corn niblets
2 tbsp. egg substitute (such as Egg Beaters)
2 tbsp. fat-free sour cream
3 tbsp. unbleached white flour

1/4 tsp. salt
1/4 tsp. black pepper
1 1/2 tbsp. canola oil, divided (butter or low-trans-fat margarine can be substituted*)

1. Place the egg whites in a small mixing bowl and beat with an electric mixer on medium speed until they hold soft peaks. Transfer the egg whites to another bowl, set aside, and add the corn to the now empty mixing bowl. Add 1 egg yolk (discard the other yolk), the egg substitute, and the sour cream; mix well on low speed or by hand.
2. Place the flour in a small bowl and stir in the salt and pepper.
3. Fold the egg whites into the corn mixture, adding a little of the flour mixture with each fold until all the batter ingredients are stirred into the corn mixture.
4. Place half of the oil in a medium nonstick frying pan over medium-high heat. When the oil is hot, add batter by slightly heaping tablespoonfuls and cook until the undersides of the fritters are nicely brown, about 2 minutes. Flip the fritters over and brown the other side, about 2–3 minutes more. Remove the cooked fritters to a plate lined with paper towels. Repeat with the remaining batter, adding the remaining oil as necessary. Enjoy as a side dish or snack!

NUTRITIONAL ANALYSES (PER SERVING)

	BEFORE	AFTER		BEFORE	AFTER
CALORIES	205	63	CHOLESTEROL	42 MG	32 MG
PROTEIN	5 G	3 G	FIBER	1 G	1 G
CARBOHYDRATES	24 G	7 G	SODIUM	338 MG	120 MG
FAT	11 G	3 G	% CALORIES FROM FAT	48	41
SATURATED FAT	2 G	1.6 G	OMEGA-3 FATTY ACIDS	N/A	0.04 G
MONOUNSATURATED FAT	N/A	0.9 G	OMEGA-6 FATTY ACIDS	N/A	0.2 G
POLYUNSATURATED FAT	N/A	0.2 G	*Nutritional analyses do not account for substitutions.		

Sweet Potato Fritters

MAKES ABOUT 10 FRITTERS

I didn't grow up with sweet potato fritters, but I do like sweet potatoes, so I was excited to try lightening up the traditional recipe. These are delicious!

1/2 c. mashed cooked sweet potatoes
    or winter squash (about 1/2 lb.,
    or 230 g, raw)
1 large egg
1/4 c. egg substitute
    (such as Egg Beaters)
1/4 c. cornmeal
1/4 c. unbleached white flour

1/4 tsp. salt
1/4 tsp. ground cinnamon
Pinch ground cayenne pepper, or more
    to taste
2 pinches ground black pepper, or more
    to taste
1/8 c. finely chopped onion (optional)
1 tbsp. canola oil

1. Add all the ingredients except the canola oil to a mixing bowl and beat on low to blend well.
2. Place a large nonstick frying pan over medium-high heat and coat the bottom with the canola oil.
3. Add batter to the hot pan by slightly heaping tablespoonfuls and cook until the undersides are nicely browned, about 2–3 minutes. Flip the fritters over and brown the other side, about 2–3 minutes more. Enjoy as a side dish or snack.

NUTRITIONAL ANALYSES (PER SERVING)

	BEFORE	AFTER		BEFORE	AFTER
CALORIES	113	58	CHOLESTEROL	49 MG	21 MG
PROTEIN	2.5 G	2 G	FIBER	1 G	1 G
CARBOHYDRATES	11 G	8 G	SODIUM	75 MG	94 MG
FAT	7 G	2 G	% CALORIES FROM FAT	56	31
SATURATED FAT	1.1 G	0.3 G	OMEGA-3 FATTY ACIDS	0.05 G	0.15 G
MONOUNSATURATED FAT	1.8 G	1 G	OMEGA-6 FATTY ACIDS	3.4 G	0.4 G
POLYUNSATURATED FAT	3.4 G	0.5 G			

Jo Jo Potato Wedges

MAKES 6 SERVINGS

Craving french fries but want something with a little more spice and flare? Jo Jo Potato Wedges taste a lot like KFC's spicy potato wedges, but they're oven fried. Try dipping them in Quick Ranch Dip (page 51), barbecue sauce, or ketchup.

2 tbsp. canola oil
1 c. unbleached or all-purpose flour
1 tsp. garlic powder
1 tsp. salt
1 tsp. ground black pepper
1/2 tsp. celery salt

1/2 tsp. seasoning salt
2 large eggs, beaten
4 medium potatoes, scrubbed and well
   rinsed
Canola cooking spray

1. Preheat the oven to 450° F (230° C). Coat the bottoms of two 9- x 13-inch baking dishes with the canola oil.
2. Combine the flour, garlic powder, salt, pepper, celery salt, and seasoning salt in a shallow dish and mix together with a fork or whisk; set aside. Place the beaten eggs in a small bowl.
3. Cut the potatoes into 1/2-inch-thick wedges. Pat them with paper towels to make sure they're nice and dry. Dip the potato wedges into the egg mixture, then dredge in the flour mixture to coat well. Place on the prepared baking dishes. Coat the tops of the potato wedges generously with canola cooking spray.
4. Bake in the center of the oven until golden brown, about 12–15 minutes.

NUTRITIONAL ANALYSES (PER 1-C. SERVING)

	BEFORE	AFTER		BEFORE	AFTER
CALORIES	384	212	CHOLESTEROL	35 MG	35 MG
PROTEIN	5 G	5 G	FIBER	3 G	3 G
CARBOHYDRATES	48 G	36 G	SODIUM	666 MG	155 MG
FAT	18 G	5.5 G	% CALORIES FROM FAT	42	23
SATURATED FAT	3.8 G	0.6 G	OMEGA-3 FATTY ACIDS	N/A	0.5 G
MONOUNSATURATED FAT	N/A	3.1 G	OMEGA-6 FATTY ACIDS	N/A	1.1 G
POLYUNSATURATED FAT	N/A	1.6 G			

Cheesy Potato Cakes with Herbed Ranch Salsa

MAKES 4 SERVINGS (2 POTATO CAKES PER SERVING)

These Cheesy Potato Cakes are a lighter version of the very popular appetizer from Claim Jumper restaurant. They're a wonderful way to use up any leftover mashed potatoes—in fact, they're so yummy, you might find yourself making extra mashed potatoes so you'll definitely have some left over. At the restaurant, the potato cakes are served with a ranch salsa, so I've included a quickie homemade version for this as well. Enjoy!

1 1/4 c. mashed potatoes
2 tbsp. grated or shredded Parmesan
    cheese
1/4 c. grated reduced-fat sharp cheddar
    cheese
1/2 c. chopped onion
1/4 tsp. dried dill weed

2 tbsp. snipped fresh chives
1/8 c. (loosely packed) chopped fresh
    cilantro (optional)
1/4 c. plain breadcrumbs
1 tbsp. canola oil
Herbed Ranch Salsa (recipe follows)

1. Place the mashed potatoes in a mixing bowl. Add the Parmesan, cheddar cheese, onion, dill, chives, and cilantro, if desired. Blend on low with an electric mixer until completely mixed. Scoop out a level 1/4 cup of the mixture and pat into a patty about 1/2 inch thick. Set on a plate and repeat with the remaining potato mixture to make about eight potato cakes.
2. Place the breadcrumbs in a small, shallow bowl. Press both sides of each potato cake into the breadcrumbs to coat well.
3. Place a large, nonstick frying pan over medium-high heat and add the canola oil. When the oil is hot, spread with a spatula to cover the bottom of the frying pan. Add the potato cakes and pan-fry for about 3–4 minutes per side, until nicely browned.
4. Remove from the heat and serve immediately with Herbed Ranch Salsa.

NUTRITIONAL ANALYSES (PER SERVING)

	BEFORE	AFTER		BEFORE	AFTER
CALORIES	307	157	CHOLESTEROL	15 MG	8 MG
PROTEIN	6 G	6 G	FIBER	2.5 G	2.5 G
CARBOHYDRATES	26 G	20 G	SODIUM	570 MG	350 MG
FAT	21 G	6 G	% CALORIES FROM FAT	62	34
SATURATED FAT	7 G	1.9 G	OMEGA-3 FATTY ACIDS	0.5 G	0.4 G
MONOUNSATURATED FAT	8 G	2.4 G	OMEGA-6 FATTY ACIDS	5 G	0.7 G
POLYUNSATURATED FAT	5.5 G	1.1 G			

Herbed Ranch Salsa

MAKES ABOUT 2/3 C.

This cool, creamy dip is great with Cheesy Potato Cakes, and also goes well with many other foods in this book.

1/3 c. fat-free or light sour cream
1 tsp. Hidden Valley Ranch dip mix
(available in a packet)

1/3 c. bottled or fresh salsa (mild, medium, or hot, depending on preference)

Place the sour cream and ranch dip mix in a small mixing bowl and beat with an electric mixer on low speed until smooth (or whisk by hand). Add in the salsa and beat until blended (or whisk in by hand).

FRY LIGHT, FRY RIGHT PREPARATION (PER SERVING)

	BEFORE	AFTER		BEFORE	AFTER
CALORIES	60	24	CHOLESTEROL	6 MG	0 MG
PROTEIN	1 G	1 G	FIBER	0.1 G	0.1 G
CARBOHYDRATES	1.4 G	4.5 G	SODIUM	231 MG	273 MG
FAT	6 G	0 G	% CALORIES FROM FAT	87	0
SATURATED FAT	1 G	N/A	OMEGA-3 FATTY ACIDS	0.3 G	0 G
MONOUNSATURATED FAT	2.6 G	N/A	OMEGA-6 FATTY ACIDS	2 G	0 G
POLYUNSATURATED FAT	2.3 G	N/A			

*Nutritional analysis does not differ significantly from traditional preparation.

Take Me Out to the Ball Game
Garlic Fries

MAKES 3 SERVINGS

Garlic fries are popular at ballparks across the country. This is a lighter rendition using a lot less oil and a lot less butter. Instead of being plunged into a vat of oil, our cut potatoes are tossed in a large zip-top bag with a small amount of canola oil, which makes them much better for you.

Canola cooking spray
1 1/2 lb. (685 g) peeled baking potatoes,
   cut into 1/4-inch-thick strips
2 tsp. canola oil
1/4 tsp. salt
1 tbsp. butter

2 1/2 tsp. minced fresh garlic
   (or 4 garlic cloves, minced)
1 tbsp. finely chopped fresh Italian or
   regular parsley
1 tbsp. freshly grated or shredded
   Parmesan cheese

1. Preheat the oven to 400° F (200° C). Coat a 9- x 13-inch baking pan with canola cooking spray.
2. In a large zip-top plastic bag, combine the potatoes with the canola oil and salt; seal the bag and toss to coat.
3. Arrange the potatoes in a single layer on the prepared baking sheet. Bake for 40–50 minutes or until tender and golden brown, turning after 20 minutes.
4. Place the butter and garlic in a large nonstick skillet over low heat. Cook for 2 minutes, stirring constantly. Add the french fries, parsley, and Parmesan cheese to the pan; toss to coat. Serve immediately.

NUTRITIONAL ANALYSES (PER SERVING)

	BEFORE	AFTER		BEFORE	AFTER
CALORIES	500	256	CHOLESTEROL	30 MG	12 MG
PROTEIN	6 G	6 G	FIBER	3.5 G	3.5 G
CARBOHYDRATES	50 G	42.3 G	SODIUM	800 MG	243 MG
FAT	30 G	7.7 G	% CALORIES FROM FAT	54	27
SATURATED FAT	11 G	3.3 G	OMEGA-3 FATTY ACIDS	1 G	1 G
MONOUNSATURATED FAT	15 G	2 G	OMEGA-6 FATTY ACIDS	2 G	1 G
POLYUNSATURATED FAT	3 G	2 G			

Easy Oven Potato Chips

MAKES 2 SERVINGS

Before I developed this recipe, I was doubtful that oven-frying would produce crispy potato chips—thankfully, I was pleasantly surprised. This recipe makes one jelly roll pan's worth of chips using a large russet potato; to increase the recipe, simply make more batches using more jelly roll pans.

Canola cooking spray
1 large russet potato

Seasonings of your choice
(such as salt to taste, seasoning salt to taste, pinch of herbs to taste, or any salt-free herb blends to taste)

1. Preheat the oven to 400° F (200° C). Coat the bottom of a 10- x 15-inch nonstick jelly roll pan with canola cooking spray.
2. Using a large, sharp, nonserrated knife, cut the potato into very thin slices—about 1/16 inch.
3. Immediately lay the potato slices flat onto the prepared pan (they should completely cover the bottom of the pan). Spray the tops with canola cooking spray and sprinkle with whichever seasonings you desire.
4. Bake for about 22–25 minutes (watching carefully). Remove the chips that have browned and crisped and continue to cook the remaining chips until they become nice and crisp, too—about 5 minutes more. Serve with your entrée or as a snack with the light or low-fat dip of your choice.

NUTRITIONAL ANALYSES (PER 2-OZ. SERVING)

	BEFORE	AFTER		BEFORE	AFTER
CALORIES	300	173	CHOLESTEROL	0 MG	0 MG
PROTEIN	4 G	4 G	FIBER	2 G	4 G
CARBOHYDRATES	30 G	37 G	SODIUM	360 MG	12 MG
FAT	20 G	1.3 G	% CALORIES FROM FAT	60	7
SATURATED FAT	6 G	0.1 G	OMEGA-3 FATTY ACIDS	2 G	0.1 G
MONOUNSATURATED FAT	3.8 G	0.7 G	OMEGA-6 FATTY ACIDS	8 G	0.3 G
POLYUNSATURATED FAT	10.2 G	0.4 G			

Oven-Fried Sweet Potato Chips

MAKES 6 SERVINGS

These chips are bright and flavorful. If you would like to use yams instead of sweet potatoes, go ahead. They'll still taste great, though yams tend to get less crisp than sweet potatoes.

Canola cooking spray

1 lb. (454 g) sweet potatoes (about 3 small to medium-sized potatoes)

1 1/2 tbsp. canola oil or olive oil

1/2 tsp. sea salt (regular salt can also be used), or more to taste

2 tsp. herb blend of choice (Italian herbs, Herbes de Provence, or any salt-free herb blend)

1. Preheat the oven to 425° F (215° C). Line a jelly roll pan or cookie sheet with foil and coat the foil with canola cooking spray (this makes cleanup easier).
2. Using a large, sharp, nonserrated knife, cut the sweet potatoes into very thin slices—about 1/8 inch.
3. Place the sweet potato slices and oil in a gallon-sized zip-top bag; seal the bag and toss to coat well.
4. Open the bag and spread the sweet potato slices evenly on the prepared jelly roll pan. Sprinkle with sea salt and herbs, if desired.
5. Bake for about 15 minutes, then flip with a spatula and bake for another 10–15 minutes or until golden brown.

NUTRITIONAL ANALYSES (PER 2-OZ. SERVING)

	BEFORE	AFTER		BEFORE	AFTER
CALORIES	228	108	CHOLESTEROL	0 MG	0 MG
PROTEIN	1.3 G	1.3 G	FIBER	2.3 G	2.3 G
CARBOHYDRATES	18.5 G	18.5 G	SODIUM	199 MG	199 MG
FAT	16 G	3.5 G	% CALORIES FROM FAT	63	29
SATURATED FAT	2 G	0.3 G	OMEGA-3 FATTY ACIDS	0.3 G	0.3 G
MONOUNSATURATED FAT	5 G	2.1 G	OMEGA-6 FATTY ACIDS	7.7 G	0.7 G
POLYUNSATURATED FAT	8 G	1.1 G			

La Poutine

MAKES 3 SERVINGS

This is a popular way to eat french fries in Quebec, which is one of my favorite places to visit. The cheese typically used to make La Poutine is not readily available in the United States, but a reduced-fat white cheddar or Monterey Jack cheese works fine. If you don't want to use frozen french fries for this recipe, just follow the recipe for Seasoned Oven Fries on page 118.

12 oz. frozen steak fries or country fries (any frozen fries with 4 g of fat or less per serving) or Seasoned Oven Fries

1/2 c. packed, shredded reduced-fat white cheddar cheese or reduced-fat Monterey Jack (about 2 oz., or 60 g)

2–4 tbsp. barbecue sauce

1. Preheat the oven to 425º F (215º C). Line a cookie sheet with foil. Spread the frozen french fries evenly on the foil.
2. Place the cookie sheet in the preheated oven and bake for 15 minutes. Remove the cookie sheet from the oven and, with a spatula, form two nests of fries.
3. Sprinkle half the cheese over each nest. Return the cookie sheet to the oven and bake until the cheese is melted, about 5 minutes.
4. Remove the cookie sheet from the oven and drizzle barbecue sauce over the top of each nest. Serve hot.

NUTRITIONAL ANALYSES (PER SERVING)

	BEFORE	AFTER		BEFORE	AFTER
CALORIES	477	212	CHOLESTEROL	20 MG	13 MG
PROTEIN	10.4 G	8 G	FIBER	1.8 G	2 G
CARBOHYDRATES	57 G	28 G	SODIUM	467 MG	264 MG
FAT	23 G	8 G	% CALORIES FROM FAT	43	34
SATURATED FAT	9.2 G	4 G	OMEGA-3 FATTY ACIDS	N/A	0 G
MONOUNSATURATED FAT	N/A	1.3 G	OMEGA-6 FATTY ACIDS	N/A	0.1 G
POLYUNSATURATED FAT	N/A	0.1 G			

Light Potato Latkes

MAKES 10 LATKES

These are delicious and really easy to make! The traditional latke recipe calls for 3 eggs and 1/2 cup peanut oil; we're using 1 egg, 6 tablespoons egg substitute, and 2 to 3 teaspoons canola oil. Serve these hot alongside roast chicken or pot roast, or on their own with applesauce, fat-free sour cream, and chopped green onions.

2 c. peeled, shredded russet potatoes, firmly packed (about 1 lb., or 454 g)
1/4 c. grated or finely chopped onion
1 large egg
6 tbsp. egg substitute (such as Egg Beaters)
2–3 tbsp. low-sodium matzo meal (make by processing 1 matzo into fine crumbs) or regular matzo meal (available in supermarkets; see note)
1 tsp. salt
2–3 tsp. canola oil
Canola cooking spray
Applesauce, fat-free sour cream, and chopped green onions, for serving (optional)

1. Place the potatoes in a cheesecloth or double thickness of paper towels and wring to extract as much water as possible.
2. In a medium bowl, combine the potatoes, onion, egg, egg substitute, matzo meal, and salt. Mix together well.
3. Place the oil in a large heavy-bottomed nonstick skillet over medium-high heat and turn to coat the bottom well. When the oil is hot, add 1/4 cup (level measure) of potato mixture, pressing it with the back of a wooden spoon to form a 1/4- to 1/2-inch-thick patty. Repeat with the remaining potato mixture. Spray the tops of the patties with canola cooking spray. Brown on one side for about 3 minutes, then turn over and brown the other side—about 3 minutes more.
4. Remove to a plate lined with paper towels. Serve hot with the entrée of your choice and applesauce, fat-free sour cream, and chopped green onions, if desired.
• NOTE: If you use regular matzo meal, delete the teaspoon of salt.

NUTRITIONAL ANALYSES (PER LATKE)

	BEFORE	AFTER		BEFORE	AFTER
CALORIES	134	74	CHOLESTEROL	90 MG	21 MG
PROTEIN	4 G	3 G	FIBER	1 G	1 G
CARBOHYDRATES	12 G	12 G	SODIUM	263 MG	260 MG
FAT	7.7 G	1.5 G	% CALORIES FROM FAT	52	19
SATURATED FAT	1.3 G	0.2 G	OMEGA-3 FATTY ACIDS	0.1 G	0.1 G
MONOUNSATURATED FAT	2.4 G	0.7 G	OMEGA-6 FATTY ACIDS	3.2 G	0.3 G
POLYUNSATURATED FAT	3.3 G	0.4 G			

Scotch Eggs

MAKES 4 SCOTCH EGGS

This is a great recipe for Easter time, when we all find ourselves up to our eyeballs in hard-boiled eggs and have had one too many egg salad sandwiches. Not only are these light Scotch Eggs a great accompaniment to a large dinner salad, they're also great for picnics.

6 oz. (170 g) turkey breakfast sausage
   (such as Jimmy Dean light sausage)
4 large hard-boiled eggs
1 tsp. crumbled dried sage
1/2 tsp. dried thyme, crumbled

1/4 tsp. ground cayenne pepper (optional)
1/2 c. all-purpose flour
1/2 c. egg substitute (such as Egg Beaters)
1 c. sourdough or French breadcrumbs
Canola cooking spray

1. Preheat the oven to 450° F (230° C). Divide the sausage into four equal portions. Place each portion on a 6-inch piece of waxed paper or plastic wrap and press into a very thin patty. Wrap each patty around a hard-boiled egg, pressing the sausage so it wraps all around the egg.
2. Place the sage, thyme, and cayenne (if desired) in a small, shallow bowl. Sprinkle evenly over each of the sausage-coated eggs.
3. Place the flour in a shallow bowl, the egg substitute in another shallow bowl, and the breadcrumbs in a third. Dredge the sausage-coated eggs first in the flour, shaking off the excess, then dip them in the egg substitute, and finally dip them in the breadcrumbs, coating them well.
4. Coat each egg with canola cooking spray. Place the eggs on a foil-lined 9-inch cake pan or baking dish and bake for about 15 minutes or until the breading is nicely browned and somewhat crisp. Let cool slightly before serving.

NUTRITIONAL ANALYSES (PER SCOTCH EGG)

	BEFORE	AFTER		BEFORE	AFTER
CALORIES	542	215	CHOLESTEROL	331 MG	246 MG
PROTEIN	21 G	20 G	FIBER	0.2 G	0.5 G
CARBOHYDRATE	10.5 G	8 G	SODIUM	727 MG	417 MG
FAT	46 G	11.5 G	% CALORIES FROM FAT	77	48
SATURATED FAT	14 G	4 G	OMEGA-3 FATTY ACIDS	N/A	0.2 G
MONOUNSATURATED FAT	17 G	5 G	OMEGA-6 FATTY ACIDS	N/A	2.3 G
POLYUNSATURATED FAT	9 G	2.5 G			

Beef Piroshkis

MAKES ABOUT 10 SERVINGS (2 PIROSHKIS PER SERVING)

This is a lightened version of a Russian recipe that appeals to kids as much as it does to grown-ups. Serve these alongside a hearty soup or salad for a nice meal, or as a snack with some fat-free sour cream.

3/4 lb. (340 g) extra-lean ground beef or
  ground sirloin
1/2 c. finely chopped onion
1 tsp. salt, divided
1/4 tsp. ground black pepper, or to taste
1/4 tsp. dried dill weed, or to taste
3 tbsp. fat-free sour cream
1 tsp. active dry yeast
2 tbsp. warm water

1/2 c. low-fat milk
1 large egg
2 tbsp. egg substitute
  (such as Egg Beaters)
2 tbsp. canola oil
2 tbsp. light corn syrup
2 c. all-purpose flour
  (plus 2 tbsp. for dusting)
Canola cooking spray

1. Place a medium skillet over medium heat. Add the ground beef and cook, breaking up with a spoon, until evenly browned. Stir in the onion and cook until soft and translucent. Sprinkle in 1/2 tsp. salt, pepper, and dill weed to taste, then stir in the fat-free sour cream. Remove from the heat and let cool.
2. Dissolve the yeast in the warm water and place in a warm location until foamy and frothy, about 10–15 minutes.
3. In a medium saucepan over low heat, warm the milk and gently whisk in the egg, egg substitute, canola oil, corn syrup, and remaining salt. Remove from the heat.
4. Place half the flour in a large mixing bowl and gradually stir in the milk mixture. Then add the yeast solution alternately with the remaining flour, stirring after each addition. Mix well. Knead on a flat surface that has been dusted with 2 tablespoons of flour, until the dough forms a ball and is not sticky. Return the dough to the bowl and cover with a clean cloth. Set in a warm location and allow to rise until about double in volume, 30 minutes to 1 hour.
5. Remove the dough from the bowl and place on a lightly floured surface. Pinch off pieces

approximately the size of golf balls. Roll the pieces into disks about 3 1/2 to 4 inches in diameter.

6. Fill the center of each disk with a heaping tablespoon of the cooled meat mixture. Fold the disks over the mixture and firmly pinch the edges to seal. Coat a nonstick jelly roll pan with canola cooking spray. Arrange the piroshkis on the pan and coat the tops with canola cooking spray. Let sit for approximately 10 minutes while you preheat the oven to 400° F (200° C).

7. Place the piroshkis in the oven and bake until golden brown, about 20 minutes. Serve hot.

NUTRITIONAL ANALYSES (PER SERVING)

	BEFORE	AFTER		BEFORE	AFTER
CALORIES	258	178	CHOLESTEROL	40 MG	40 MG
PROTEIN	11 G	11 G	FIBER	1 G	1 G
CARBOHYDRATES	22 G	22 G	SODIUM	280 MG	280 MG
FAT	14 G	5 G	% CALORIES FROM FAT	49	25
SATURATED FAT	2.3 G	1 1 G	OMEGA-3 FATTY ACIDS	0.4 G	0.3 G
MONOUNSATURATED FAT	4.7 G	2.5 G	OMEGA-6 FATTY ACIDS	5.9 G	0.6 G
POLYUNSATURATED FAT	6.4 G	1.1 G			

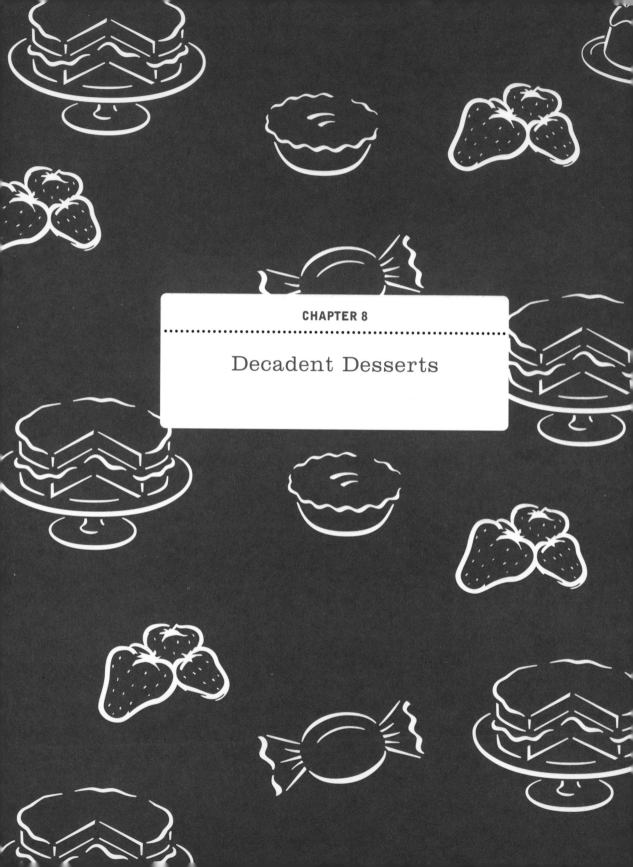

CHAPTER 8

Decadent Desserts

Devil's Food Cake Doughnuts

MAKES ABOUT 12 DOUGHNUTS

Thank goodness for doughnut pans—they make these light chocolate doughnuts possible. You can find doughnut pans at superstores like Target, and at many kitchen and crafts stores. The pans enable you to bake your batter in the shape of a doughnut instead of deep-frying it. You can serve these nude or topped with powdered sugar or the Vanilla Glaze on page 161.

1 1/2 c. unbleached white flour
1 c. granulated sugar
1/4 c. unsweetened cocoa powder
1 tsp. baking soda
1/2 tsp. salt
1 c. water

2 tbsp. canola oil (plus more oil for
   preparing pans)
3 tbsp. fat-free sour cream (light sour
   cream can be substituted*)
1 tbsp. vinegar
1 1/2 tsp. vanilla extract

1. Preheat the oven to 350° F (175° C). Using a pastry brush, lightly coat the doughnut cups with canola oil.
2. In a large bowl, combine the flour, sugar, cocoa, baking soda, and salt; mix well. Add the water, canola oil, sour cream, vinegar, and vanilla. Beat with an electric mixer on medium speed for 2 minutes.
3. Fill the prepared doughnut cups almost to the top (if you're using Donut Express brand pans, this will mean about 1/4 cup of batter per doughnut). Bake until cooked through, about 10 minutes. Let cool before removing from the pan and/or glazing.

NUTRITIONAL ANALYSES (PER 2 UNFROSTED DOUGHNUTS)

	BEFORE	AFTER		BEFORE	AFTER
CALORIES	520	286	CHOLESTEROL	0 MG	1 MG
PROTEIN	6 G	4 G	FIBER	1 G	2 G
CARBOHYDRATE	60 G	57 G	SODIUM	560 MG	410 MG
FAT	28 G	5.3 G	% CALORIES FROM FAT	48	17
SATURATED FAT	6 G	0.7 G	OMEGA-3 FATTY ACIDS	N/A	0.4 G
MONOUNSATURATED FAT	N/A	3 G	OMEGA-6 FATTY ACIDS	N/A	1 G
POLYUNSATURATED FAT	N/A	1.4 G	*Nutritional analyses do not account for substitutions.		

Old-Fashioned Applesauce Doughnut Cakes

MAKES ABOUT 10 DOUGHNUT CAKES

This is an old-fashioned doughnut recipe that we're baking in mini angel food cake pans (though doughnut pans can also be used) instead of deep-fat frying. The cakes are simple and delicious.

Canola cooking spray
2 1/4 c. unbleached white flour
1 1/2 tsp. baking powder
1/2 tsp. baking soda
1/2 tsp. ground cinnamon
1/2 tsp. ground nutmeg
1/4 tsp. ground cloves
1/4 tsp. salt
1/2 c. granulated sugar
1/4 c. packed brown sugar

1 large egg
1/4 c. egg substitute (such as Egg Beaters)
2 tbsp. canola oil
1/4 c. fat-free half-and-half (low-fat milk
   can be substituted*)
1/4 c. low-fat buttermilk
1 c. unsweetened applesauce
1/2 tsp. vanilla extract
Powdered sugar, for dusting (optional)

1. Preheat the oven to 375º F (190º C). Coat two mini angel food cake or doughnut pans with canola cooking spray.
2. Stir together the flour, baking powder, baking soda, spices, and salt in a medium bowl.
3. Place the sugar, brown sugar, egg, and egg substitute in a mixing bowl and beat with an electric mixer on medium speed until fluffy. Beat in the canola oil until just blended.
4. Add the flour mixture to the egg mixture, alternating with the half-and-half and buttermilk, beginning and ending with the dry ingredients. Beat until well blended. Stir in the applesauce and vanilla extract and beat on low until combined.
5. Fill each mini angel food cake or doughnut cup with about 1/2 cup of batter. Bake until the cake tops bounce back when touched lightly, about 15 minutes.
6. Remove the mini doughnut cakes from the pans and let cool. Dust with powdered sugar if desired.

NUTRITIONAL ANALYSES (PER SERVING, WITHOUT POWDERED SUGAR)

	BEFORE	AFTER		BEFORE	AFTER
CALORIES	250	202	CHOLESTEROL	28 MG	22 MG
PROTEIN	4 G	5 G	FIBER	1 G	1 G
CARBOHYDRATE	31 G	38 G	SODIUM	250 MG	216 MG
FAT	10 G	3.4 G	% CALORIES FROM FAT	36	15
SATURATED FAT	2.5 G	0.4 G	OMEGA-3 FATTY ACIDS	N/A	0.3 G
MONOUNSATURATED FAT	N/A	1.9 G	OMEGA-6 FATTY ACIDS	N/A	0.6 G
POLYUNSATURATED FAT	N/A	0.9 G	*Nutritional analyses do not account for substitutions.		

Jelly Doughnut Muffins
with **Vanilla Glaze**

MAKES 16 DOUGHNUTS

These breakfast gems are a delightful cross between a fried jelly doughnut and a moist muffin. Fill them with your favorite jelly (mine is boysenberry).

1 c. milk
4 1/2 tbsp. canola oil, divided
1/4 c. light cream cheese
1/3 c. sugar
1 tsp. salt
2 large eggs

3 c. unbleached white flour (1/2 c. more if needed in kneading step)
1 package active dry yeast
1/2 c. jelly of your choice (boysenberry, raspberry, and cherry work well)

1. Place the milk in a microwave-safe glass and warm in the microwave on high until fairly hot to the touch, about 1 minute. (Or place the milk in a small saucepan over low heat and cook until just hot.)
2. Place 2 tablespoons of the canola oil along with the cream cheese, sugar, and salt in a large mixing bowl and beat with an electric mixer on low until blended. Slowly pour the hot milk over the cream cheese mixture and continue to beat until well blended.
3. Add the eggs one at a time, beating well after each addition.
4. Stir together 2 cups of the flour and the yeast in a large bowl. Add the flour mixture slowly to the milk mixture and beat on low until smooth. Beat in the remaining flour to make a soft dough. Turn the dough onto a well-floured surface and knead until smooth and elastic, about 5 minutes.
5. Place the dough in a large mixing bowl that has been lightly coated with canola oil or canola margarine. Turn the dough over to coat the entire surface with oil. Cover bowl and let dough rise in a warm place until doubled, about 1 1/4 hours.
6. Add 1/2 teaspoon of the canola oil to the bottom of each of 16 muffin cups. Punch down

NUTRITIONAL ANALYSES (PER DOUGHNUT WITHOUT GLAZE)

	BEFORE	AFTER		BEFORE	AFTER
CALORIES	240	182	CHOLESTEROL	30 MG	29 MG
PROTEIN	4 G	4 G	FIBER	1 G	1 G
CARBOHYDRATE	32 G	30 G	SODIUM	260 MG	174 MG
FAT	10 G	5 G	% CALORIES FROM FAT	38	27
SATURATED FAT	2.5 G	0.8 G	OMEGA-3 FATTY ACIDS	N/A	0.4 G
MONOUNSATURATED FAT	N/A	2.6 G	OMEGA-6 FATTY ACIDS	N/A	0.9
POLYUNSATURATED FAT	N/A	1.3 G			

the dough and split it into 16 equal-sized balls (about the size of golf balls). Using your hands, press each ball into a 1/2-inch-thick circle, then spoon 1 1/2 teaspoons of jelly in the middle. Bring up all the sides of the dough to wrap up the jelly, squeezing the dough ends together well to seal. Place each ball in a muffin cup and roll around to cover the entire surface with oil.

7. Let rise in a warm place until almost double in size, about 30 minutes. Preheat the oven to 375° F (190° C). Place the muffin tin in the oven and bake for about 15–18 minutes or until the tops of the doughnut muffins are nicely browned. Remove from the oven to cool. While the doughnuts cool, prepare the Vanilla Glaze.

Vanilla Glaze

MAKES 3/4 C.

1 c. powdered sugar   1/2 tsp. vanilla extract
2 tsp. water

Combine the powdered sugar, water, and vanilla extract in a small bowl and stir until smooth. Roll each cooled doughnut muffin in the glaze to coat. Enjoy!

FRY LIGHT, FRY RIGHT PREPARATION (PER SERVING) *

CALORIES	20 G	CHOLESTEROL	0 MG
PROTEIN	0 G	FIBER	0 G
CARBOHYDRATE	5 G	SODIUM	0 MG
FAT	0 G	% CALORIES FROM FAT	0
SATURATED FAT	N/A	OMEGA-3 FATTY ACIDS	N/A
MONOUNSATURATED FAT	N/A	OMEGA-6 FATTY ACIDS	N/A
POLYUNSATURATED FAT	N/A	*Nutritional analysis does not differ significantly from traditional preparation.	

Braided Apple Fritter Bread

MAKES 16 SERVINGS

This is as yummy as it is beautiful. The sautéed apples offer a nice surprise in every bite, and the apple-cinnamon glaze tops it off perfectly.

1 tbsp. butter
3 c. diced peeled tart apples
   (about 2 large apples)
1/2 c. apple juice
2 tbsp. plus 2/3 c. sugar, divided
1 tsp. ground cinnamon
4 1/2 c. unbleached flour, divided, plus
   more for kneading
1 tsp. salt
4 tsp. active dry yeast

1 c. plus 2 tbsp. low-fat milk
3 tbsp. butter
1 egg, lightly beaten
1/4 c. egg substitute
   (such as Egg Beaters)
Canola cooking spray
1 1/2 c. powdered sugar
4 tsp. melted butter
4 tsp. concentrated apple juice
2–4 pinches of ground cinnamon

1. Start melting 1 tablespoon of butter in a large nonstick frying pan. Add the apples and sauté for 3 minutes, stirring frequently. Stir in the apple juice, 2 tablespoons of the sugar, and the cinnamon and simmer for 3 minutes longer; set aside to cool.
2. In a large mixing bowl, combine the remaining sugar with the flour, salt, and yeast. Set aside.
3. In a small saucepan over low heat, combine the milk and 3 tablespoons of butter; cook, stirring constantly, until just warm to the touch and the butter is just melted.
4. Add the milk mixture to the flour mixture and beat with an electric mixer on low for 30 seconds. Add the egg and egg substitute and beat on low for 30 seconds, stopping to scrape the sides of the bowl. Beat on medium-high speed for 2 minutes. Then beat in the apple mixture on low speed, adding more flour until the dough is too stiff to beat.
5. Turn the dough out onto a well-floured surface and knead in enough of the remaining flour to make a moderately stiff dough—about 3 minutes.
6. Shape into two balls and let rest for 15 minutes. Meanwhile, coat a cookie sheet with canola cooking spray.

7. Divide each ball into three pieces. Roll each piece into a rope about 1 inch wide and 12 inches long. Press three ropes together at one end and place on the prepared cookie sheet. Braid the three ropes and press the ends together. Repeat with the remaining dough. Let the braids rise at room temperature for an hour or in the refrigerator overnight. Preheat the oven to 400° F (200° C).

9. Bake the braids until light brown on top and cooked through, about 25 minutes. While the braids bake, prepare the Apple Glaze: Beat together the powdered sugar, melted butter, apple juice, and cinnamon with an electric mixer until smooth. When the braids come out of the oven, coat each generously with glaze.

NUTRITIONAL ANALYSES (PER SERVING)

	BEFORE	AFTER		BEFORE	AFTER
CALORIES	300	256	CHOLESTEROL	0 MG	24 MG
PROTEIN	4 G	5 G	FIBER	1 G	2 G
CARBOHYDRATE	41 G	49 G	SODIUM	360 MG	205 MG
FAT	14 G	4.5 G	% CALORIES FROM FAT	42	16
SATURATED FAT	3 G	2.6 G	OMEGA-3 FATTY ACIDS	N/A	0.06 G
MONOUNSATURATED FAT	N/A	1.3 G	OMEGA-6 FATTY ACIDS	N/A	0.15 G
POLYUNSATURATED FAT	N/A	0.2 G			

Mini Funnel Cakes with Strawberry Grand Marnier Cream

MAKES ABOUT 18 MINI CAKES

Sadly, there's really no way to make funnel cakes as we know and love them without frying the batter in a tub of boiling fat. But what we can do is bake the exact same funnel cake batter into mini cakes and top them with the goodies we love on funnel cakes. My favorite funnel cake topping is Strawberry Grand Marnier Cream—I've included a recipe for that, too!

1/2 tbsp. canola oil
    (for brushing the pans)
3/4 c. low-fat milk
1/2 tsp. vanilla extract
1 large egg
1 1/3 c. unbleached white flour
3 tbsp. granulated sugar

1/4 tsp. ground cinnamon
1 tsp. baking soda
3/4 tsp. baking powder
1/4 tsp. salt
Strawberry Grand Marnier Cream (recipe
    follows) or powdered sugar, for serving
    (optional)

1. Preheat the oven to 425° F (215° C). Brush the insides of 18 muffin cups with canola oil.
2. Place the milk, vanilla, and egg in a mixing bowl and beat with an electric mixer on medium speed until well blended. Add the flour, sugar, cinnamon, baking soda, baking powder, and salt; beat on low until a smooth batter forms.
3. Place the muffin pans in the oven for 3 minutes to heat. When the pans are hot, quickly spoon 1 tablespoon of batter into each muffin cup. Spray the tops of each cake lightly with canola cooking spray and bake for 8–9 minutes.
4. Remove the pans from the oven and let cool slightly. Remove the mini cakes from the muffin cups and cut them open. Top each with a spoon of Strawberry Grand Marnier Cream or dust with powdered sugar. Serve warm.

NUTRITIONAL ANALYSES (PER MINI CAKE, WITHOUT CREAM)

	BEFORE	AFTER		BEFORE	AFTER
CALORIES	150	50	CHOLESTEROL	30 MG	12 MG
PROTEIN	3 G	2 G	FIBER	0.4 G	0.2 G
CARBOHYDRATE	15 G	9 G	SODIUM	100 MG	128 MG
FAT	7 G	1 G	% CALORIES FROM FAT	42	14
SATURATED FAT	1.5 G	0.2 G	OMEGA-3 FATTY ACIDS	0.3 G	0.05 G
MONOUNSATURATED FAT	2.5 G	0.4 G	OMEGA-6 FATTY ACIDS	2.6 G	0.1 G
POLYUNSATURATED FAT	3 G	0.2 G			

Strawberry Grand Marnier Cream

MAKES 1 1/2 C. (ABOUT 12 DOLLOPS)

This topping also works wonderfully with a light pound cake, angel food cake, or even waffles.

1 c. Cool Whip Lite (or similar low-fat whipped topping)

1 c. unsweetened, hulled, sliced fresh strawberries (frozen variety okay in a pinch)

1–2 tsp. Grand Marnier, to taste

Stir together the Cool Whip, the strawberry slices, and 1 teaspoon of the Grand Marnier in a medium-sized serving bowl. Add another teaspoon of liqueur if you'd prefer a stronger orange flavor. Serve immediately or cover and store in the refrigerator for 1–2 days.

NUTRITIONAL ANALYSES (PER DOLLOP)

	BEFORE	AFTER		BEFORE	AFTER
CALORIES	41	20	CHOLESTEROL	14 MG	0 MG
PROTEIN	0.3 G	0.1 G	FIBER	0.2 G	0.3 G
CARBOHYDRATE	1.6 G	2.6 G	SODIUM	4 MG	0.2 MG
FAT	4 G	0.7 G	% CALORIES FROM FAT	82	31
SATURATED FAT	2.3 G	0.7 G	OMEGA-3 FATTY ACIDS	N/A	0.01 G
MONOUNSATURATED FAT	1 G	0.01 G	OMEGA-6 FATTY ACIDS	N/A	0.01 G
POLYUNSATURATED FAT	0.2 G	0.03 G			

Honey-Glazed Loukoumades

MAKES ABOUT 10 SERVINGS (3 PUFFS PER SERVING)

These Greek puff pastries are normally deep-fried (like a doughnut hole), then glazed with honey. For our version, we've lightened things up considerably: We use half the amount of butter in the dough, coat the loukoumades with a little bit of canola oil and let them rise naturally (instead of in a vat of oil), and finally bake them until they're brown and puffy. These loukamades do look different, but they still taste great!

2 packages active dry yeast (3 3/4 tsp.)
1/2 c. warm water
    (105–115° F, or 40–46° C)
1 c. warm low-fat milk (105–115° F, or
    40–46° C)
1/4 c. granulated sugar
1 tsp. salt
1 large egg beaten with 1/4 c. egg
    substitute (such as Egg Beaters)

1/4 c. butter or low-trans-fat margarine,
    melted and cooled
2 tsp. finely chopped orange zest
    (optional)
4 c. unbleached white flour
Canola cooking spray
1–2 tbsp. canola oil
5 tbsp. honey
1 tsp. ground cinnamon, or more to taste

1. In a small bowl, sprinkle the yeast over the warm water and let stand to soften and foam up, about 5 minutes.
2. Pour the milk into a large bowl and use an electric mixer on low speed to blend in the sugar and salt. Stir in the yeast mixture and the egg mixture. Then add the melted butter and orange zest and beat well on low. Slowly add 4 cups of flour while continuing to beat on low speed. The batter should be smooth and sticky.
3. Preheat the oven to 375° F (190° C). Coat a 10- x 15-inch nonstick jelly roll pan with canola cooking spray. Keep your hands well coated with the 1–2 tablespoons of oil as you break the dough into tablespoon-sized pieces and place them on the prepared jelly roll pan. (Make sure the dough balls are lightly coated with oil from your hands; add more oil to your hands as needed.)

4. Let the dough rise on top of the stove (or cover with a sheet of waxed paper and let rise in a warm place) until double in size, about 30–45 minutes. Bake until nicely brown on all sides, about 12 minutes.
5. While the bread puffs are baking, add the honey to a small saucepan and heat over low heat until warm (you can also add the honey to a microwave-safe bowl and microwave on low until it's warm and pourable, about 2 minutes).
6. Layer some of the bread puffs on a serving platter, drizzle with honey, and dust with cinnamon. Top this with another layer of bread puffs and repeat with the honey and cinnamon.

NUTRITIONAL ANALYSES (PER SERVING)

	BEFORE	AFTER		BEFORE	AFTER
CALORIES	399	296	CHOLESTEROL	77 MG	35 MG
PROTEIN	8 G	8 G	FIBER	2 G	1.5 G
CARBOHYDRATE	54 G	49 G	SODIUM	354 MG	289 MG
FAT	17 G	7 G	% CALORIES FROM FAT	38	21
SATURATED FAT	7.3 G	3.3 G	OMEGA-3 FATTY ACIDS	0.2 G	0.3 G
MONOUNSATURATED FAT	4.8 G	2.8 G	OMEGA-6 FATTY ACIDS	3.7 G	0.6 G
POLYUNSATURATED FAT	4 G	0.9 G			

Mexican Buñuelos

MAKES ABOUT 8 SERVINGS (2 BUÑUELOS PER SERVING)

Buñuelos are yummy, crispy, Mexican flat sweet breads that are usually deep-fried and sprinkled with cinnamon sugar. We make lower-cholesterol dough using half the eggs called for and replace the rest with egg substitute. These are also pan-fried in a nonstick skillet with a little bit of canola oil instead of being deep-fried in lard or shortening.

2 large eggs
1/2 c. egg substitute (such as Egg
    Beaters)
1/4 c. white sugar
4 tsp. canola oil, divided

2 1/2 c. all-purpose flour, divided
1 tsp. baking powder
1 tsp. salt
1/4 c. white sugar
1 tsp. ground cinnamon

1. In a large bowl, combine the eggs, egg substitute, and sugar and beat with an electric mixer on medium speed until thick and lemon colored. Stir in 1 teaspoon of the canola oil.
2. In a separate bowl, stir together 2 cups of the flour with the baking powder and salt. Gradually add this to the egg mixture and beat well.
3. Turn the dough out onto a well-floured board (use the remaining 1/2 cup flour, and more if needed) and knead thoroughly until the dough is smooth. Shape into 16 balls. Dust a rolling pin with flour and roll out each dough ball into a circle about 4 to 5 inches in diameter; place on a piece of waxed paper. Let stand uncovered for about 10 minutes.
4. Place a large nonstick skillet over medium-high heat. Lightly brush the tops of the flat breads with canola oil then add them, oil-side down, to the skillet (about four per batch). While the buñuelos cook, brush the tops lightly with canola oil. When the bottoms are golden (about 2 minutes), flip the buñuelos and brown the other side, about 1 minute more. Remove them to a plate and sprinkle with a mixture of the cinnamon and sugar. Serve warm.

NUTRITIONAL ANALYSES (PER SERVING)

	BEFORE	AFTER		BEFORE	AFTER
CALORIES	326	241	CHOLESTEROL	123 MG	61 MG
PROTEIN	8 G	7.4 G	FIBER	1 G	1 G
CARBOHYDRATE	43 G	43 G	SODIUM	388 MG	388 MG
FAT	14 G	4.3 G	% CALORIES FROM FAT	39	16
SATURATED FAT	2.3 G	0.7 G	OMEGA-3 FATTY ACIDS	0.1 G	0.2 G
MONOUNSATURATED FAT	3.7 G	2 G	OMEGA-6 FATTY ACIDS	6.5 G	0.8 G
POLYUNSATURATED FAT	6.6 G	1.1 G			

Cinnamon Stix

MAKES 8 CINNAMON STIX (1 PER SERVING)

These are reminiscent of those wonderful, flaky, cinnamon pastries you can buy at bakeries. Our version is much healthier since we're using lower-fat dough and no-trans-fat margarine to coat the sticks before sprinkling them with a cinnamon mixture. But guess what? These still turn out flaky and totally delicious.

Canola cooking spray
1 1/2 tbsp. no-trans-fat margarine (butter
   can be substituted*)
1/2 tsp. vanilla extract
3 tbsp. granulated sugar

1 tsp. ground cinnamon
1 8-oz. (227 g.) tube reduced-fat crescent
   rolls (found in refrigerated section of
   supermarket)

1. Preheat the oven to 400° F (200° C). Coat a cookie sheet with canola cooking spray.
2. Place the margarine in a small microwave-safe bowl and microwave briefly to melt. (Or place the margarine in a small saucepan over low heat until melted.) Stir in the vanilla extract. In another small bowl, stir the sugar and cinnamon together until well blended.
3. Unfold the crescent roll dough and separate it into eight triangles. Brush the tops of the triangles with a little more than half of the vanilla-margarine mixture and sprinkle lightly with half of the cinnamon mixture. Then fold in the two long corners of each triangle to form a small rectangle. Roll the rectangles into cylinders, starting at the long edge where the dough layers are separated and ending at the long edge where the dough is folded. Twist the cylinders a few times while stretching them into 6-inch-long sticks. Place the twists on the prepared cookie sheet.
4. Brush the tops of the twists with the remaining margarine mixture and sprinkle carefully with the remaining cinnamon mixture. Bake until golden brown, about 10 minutes.

NUTRITIONAL ANALYSES (PER SERVING)

	BEFORE	AFTER		BEFORE	AFTER
CALORIES	213	137	CHOLESTEROL	11 MG	0 MG
PROTEIN	3.7 G	2 G	FIBER	0.6 G	1 G
CARBOHYDRATE	23 G	17 G	SODIUM	199 MG	247 MG
FAT	12 G	6.5 G	% CALORIES FROM FAT	51	43
SATURATED FAT	3 G	1.3 G	OMEGA-3 FATTY ACIDS	0.1 G	0.1 G
MONOUNSATURATED FAT	6.6 G	1 G	OMEGA-6 FATTY ACIDS	1.5 G	0.5 G
POLYUNSATURATED FAT	1.6 G	0.6 G	*Nutritional analyses do not account for substitutions.		

Peach Pie Mini Turnovers

MAKES ABOUT 12 SERVINGS (2 TURNOVERS PER SERVING)

I know baked pie turnovers aren't exactly the same as their fried cousins, but they're still delicious! I've lowered the fat in the pastry crust and kept the turnovers healthy by baking them instead of frying them (as some recipes suggest). The peach filling is wonderful, and you can brush the turnovers with a little melted butter (or no-trans-fat margarine) and sprinkle them with sugar, if you'd like.

Canola cooking spray
1 16-oz. (454 g) bag frozen peaches,
   partially thawed and coarsely diced
   (about 3 c. diced)
6 tbsp. plus 2 tsp. granulated sugar,
   divided
1 tbsp. lemon juice
1/2 tsp. ground cinnamon
3 c. unbleached white flour
   (plus more for rolling dough)

1/2 tsp. salt
5 tbsp. canola oil
4–5 tbsp. low-fat buttermilk
1 tbsp. melted butter or no-trans-fat
   margarine, for topping (optional)
Cinnamon sugar (2 tbsp. granulated
   sugar mixed with 1/2 tsp. ground
   cinnamon), for topping (optional)

1. Preheat the oven to 400° F (200° C). Coat a nonstick cookie sheet or jelly roll pan with canola cooking spray; set aside.
2. Place the diced peaches, 6 tablespoons of the granulated sugar, the lemon juice, and the cinnamon in a nonstick medium saucepan and stir well. Cook over low to medium heat, stirring occasionally, for 10 minutes. Crush the peaches with a potato masher and continue to cook over low-medium heat for 3–4 minutes more until the mixture looks like chunky applesauce and the liquid is very thick. Pour into a bowl to cool.
3. While the peach filling is cooling, make the pastry crust: Place the flour, the remaining 2 teaspoons granulated sugar, the salt, the canola oil, and 4 tablespoons of the buttermilk in a mixing bowl and beat with an electric mixer on low until just blended. Add an additional tablespoon of buttermilk if needed. Use your hands to gather the pastry into a ball.

4. Lay a sheet of waxed paper on a flat surface and dust lightly with flour. Dust a rolling pin with flour and roll out the pastry dough on the floured waxed paper until it's thin (like a piecrust). Use a 3-inch round cutter to cut circles from the dough (I like to use a 3-inch cut-and-seal device from Pampered Chef for this).
5. Add a scant tablespoon of peach filling to the center of each circle and fold over to make a half circle. You can use the cut-and-seal device to seal the edges, or use your fingers or the tongs of a fork. Brush the tops of the turnovers with melted butter and sprinkle lightly with cinnamon sugar, if desired.
6. Place in the oven and bake until the pastry is golden brown, about 18 minutes.

NUTRITIONAL ANALYSES (PER 2 MINI TURNOVERS)

	BEFORE	AFTER		BEFORE	AFTER
CALORIES	350	197	CHOLESTEROL	0 MG	0.3 MG
PROTEIN	5 G	3.5 G	FIBER	2 G	2 MG
CARBOHYDRATE	49 G	32.5 G	SODIUM	340 MG	102 MG
FAT	15 G	6 G	% CALORIES FROM FAT	39	27
SATURATED FAT	4 G	0.5 G	OMEGA-3 FATTY ACIDS	N/A	0.5 G
MONOUNSATURATED FAT	N/A	3.5 G	OMEGA-6 FATTY ACIDS	N/A	1.2 G
POLYUNSATURATED FAT	N/A	1.7 G			

Mango Chimichangas
with Raspberry Dipping Sauces

MAKES 8 SMALL-SIZED CHIMICHANGAS (OR 4 LARGE)

I know it seems a little strange to see the words mango and chimichanga in the same recipe title, but everyone who tries this fun dessert loves it! Instead of deep-frying these, you'll use very fresh tortillas and bake them in the oven until crispy. When I make these, I go to a nearby Mexican restaurant and order a dozen flour tortillas freshly made. If you don't have this option, just try to find the freshest flour tortillas possible from your supermarket (check the sell-by dates on the package).

Canola cooking spray
4 c. diced fresh or frozen mango (dice should be 1/2 inch; if using frozen mango, thaw slightly and cut to correct size)
1/3 c. granulated sugar
1 tbsp. lime juice
2 tsp. cornstarch

8 6-inch or 4 10-inch very fresh flour tortillas
Powdered sugar, for dusting before serving
Super Quick Raspberry Sauce or Fresh Raspberry Sauce, for serving (recipes follow)

1. Preheat the oven to 400)° F (200° C). Coat the bottom of a nonstick 9- x 13-inch baking dish or cookie sheet generously with canola cooking spray.
2. In a medium-sized bowl, combine the mango, sugar, lime juice, and cornstarch. Toss to blend well.
3. Place the tortillas in the microwave and heat on high for about 30–60 seconds to make them nice and soft. (Or place them in a nonstick pan over low heat until soft.)
4. Spoon about 1/2 cup of the mango mixture into the center of one of the tortillas. Fold up the bottom of the tortilla, then fold the sides in toward the center and roll up into a burrito

NUTRITIONAL ANALYSES (PER SMALL CHIMICHANGA WITHOUT SAUCE)

	BEFORE	AFTER		BEFORE	AFTER
CALORIES	235	192	CHOLESTEROL	0.1 MG	0 MG
PROTEIN	2.5 G	3.5 G	FIBER	2.6 G	3 G
CARBOHYDRATE	28 G	40 G	SODIUM	134 G	154 MG
FAT	13 G	2.5 G	% CALORIES FROM FAT	50	12
SATURATED FAT	3 G	0.6 G	OMEGA-3 FATTY ACIDS	0.3 G	0.1 G
MONOUNSATURATED FAT	5 G	1.3 G	OMEGA-6 FATTY ACIDS	3.6 G	0.3 G
POLYUNSATURATED FAT	4 G	0.4 G			

shape. Place seam-side down in the prepared pan. Repeat with the remaining mango filling and tortillas, making sure the chimichangas are nicely spread out in the pan. (If you like, you can use a wooden toothpick to keep each chimichanga rolled up.)

5. Spray the tops of the chimichangas with canola cooking spray. Bake for 15 minutes or until the tortillas begin to get crispy. Remove from the oven and turn on the broiler.

6. Place the chimichangas under the broiler, about 8 inches from the heating unit, for about 1 minute or until the tops are golden brown. Remove to plates.

7. Dust the tops of the chimichangas with powdered sugar and serve hot with a healthy drizzle of the raspberry sauce of your choice.

Super Quick Raspberry Sauce

MAKES 8 SERVINGS

**1/3 c. gourmet raspberry
jam or preserves**

Place the jam in a microwave-safe serving dish and warm in the microwave for about 1 minute on high to soften into a sauce.

FRY LIGHT, FRY RIGHT PREPARATION (PER 2 TSP.)*

CALORIES	33	FIBER	0 G
PROTEIN	0 G	SODIUM	0 MG
CARBOHYDRATE	9 G	% CALORIES FROM FAT	0
FAT	0 G	OMEGA-3 FATTY ACIDS	0 G
SATURATED FAT	N/A	OMEGA-6 FATTY ACIDS	0 G
MONOUNSATURATED FAT	N/A		
POLYUNSATURATED FAT	N/A	*Nutritional analysis does not differ significantly	
CHOLESTEROL	0 MG	from traditional preparation.	

Fresh Raspberry Sauce

MAKES 8 SERVINGS

1 c. fresh or frozen unsweetened
   raspberries
2 tbsp. sugar

2 tbsp. raspberry liqueur
   (such as Chambord)
2 tbsp. orange juice

Combine the ingredients in a blender or food processor and puree or pulse until well blended. Serve "as is" if you don't mind seeds, or strain through a nonreactive sieve to remove the seeds.

FRY LIGHT, FRY RIGHT PREPARATION (PER 1 TBSP)*

CALORIES	36	FIBER	1 G
PROTEIN	0.2 G	SODIUM	0.4 MG
CARBOHYDRATE	7.5 G	% CALORIES FROM FAT	2
FAT	0.1 G	OMEGA-3 FATTY ACIDS	0.02 G
SATURATED FAT	0.01 G	OMEGA-6 FATTY ACIDS	0.04 G
MONOUNSATURATED FAT	0.01 G		
POLYUNSATURATED FAT	0.05 G	*Nutritional analysis does not differ significantly	
CHOLESTEROL	0 MG	from traditional preparation.	

Spiced Apple Cider Fritters

MAKES ABOUT 4 SERVINGS (3 FRITTERS PER SERVING)

My parents were from Holland, where making apple fritters is a New Year's tradition, so I grew up with these sweet treats. For this light version, we're using apple rings instead of wedges, which makes it easier to pan-fry the fritters in just a touch of oil.

2/3 c. unbleached white flour

1/2 tsp. apple pie spice (pumpkin pie spice can be used in a pinch)

1/8 tsp. baking soda

1/8 tsp. salt

9 tbsp. spiced apple cider (available in some supermarkets; or heat 1 c. cider with a cinnamon stick and a few cloves on low heat for 10 minutes)

1 tbsp. canola oil

2 large Golden Delicious or Fuji apples, cored, peeled, and sliced into 1/4- to 1/3-inch-thick rings

2 tbsp. powdered sugar, for serving

1. Place the flour, apple pie spice, baking soda, and salt in a mixing bowl; beat with an electric mixer on low speed to blend well. Add the apple cider and beat on low until a smooth batter forms.
2. Place a large, nonstick skillet over medium-high heat and add the canola oil; tilt the pan to coat the bottom evenly with the oil.
3. When the oil is hot, quickly dip the apple rings one at a time into the batter and immediately transfer to the pan. Let brown on the bottom for about 2–3 minutes. Flip the apple slices to lightly brown the other side, about 2–3 minutes more. When the fritters are done, use a fork to remove them to a serving plate lined with paper towels.
4. Dust the tops of the apple fritters with powdered sugar and serve. Happy New Year!

NUTRITIONAL ANALYSES (PER SERVING)

	BEFORE	AFTER		BEFORE	AFTER
CALORIES	366	206	CHOLESTEROL	0 MG	0 MG
PROTEIN	3 G	3 G	FIBER	3 G	3 G
CARBOHYDRATE	41 G	41 G	SODIUM	111 MG	111 MG
FAT	22 G	4 G	% CALORIES FROM FAT	54	13
SATURATED FAT	2.6 G	0.3 G	OMEGA-3 FATTY ACIDS	0.5 G	0.4 G
MONOUNSATURATED FAT	6.5 G	2.1 G	OMEGA-6 FATTY ACIDS	11.3 G	0.8 G
POLYUNSATURATED FAT	11.8 G	1.2 G			

Cinnamon Crisps

MAKES 6 SERVINGS

When you deep-fry flour tortillas, they get all nice and golden and crunchy. But this crispiness comes at a cost—lots of calories and fat grams. In this light recipe, we're brushing a little bit of butter onto flour tortilla triangles and sprinkling cinnamon sugar over the top. Baking the tortillas in the oven creates the near crispiness of the deep-fried version, but without as much fat and calories.

Canola cooking spray
6 8-inch flour tortillas
2 tbsp. no- or low-trans fat margarine
   (with 8 grams of fat or less per
   tablespoon)

1/2 tsp. ground cinnamon
2 tbsp. sugar

1. Preheat the oven to 350° F (175° C). Coat two nonstick jelly roll pans (or similar) with canola cooking spray. Cut each tortilla into eight wedges.
2. Brush the tops of the tortilla wedges lightly with melted butter and sprinkle carefully with a mixture of the cinnamon and sugar.
3. Bake in the center of the oven until crispy, about 12–15 minutes.

NUTRITIONAL ANALYSES (PER SERVING)

	BEFORE	AFTER		BEFORE	AFTER
CALORIES	230	157	CHOLESTEROL	0 MG	0 MG
PROTEIN	4 G	3 G	FIBER	1 G	1 G
CARBOHYDRATE	28 G	24 G	SODIUM	203 MG	194 MG
FAT	11 G	5 G	% CALORIES FROM FAT	43	28
SATURATED FAT	2.4 G	0.8 G	OMEGA-3 FATTY ACIDS	N/A	0.4 G
MONOUNSATURATED FAT	N/A	2 G	OMEGA-6 FATTY ACIDS	N/A	1.8 G
POLYUNSATURATED FAT	N/A	2.2 G			

Glazed Spiced Walnuts

MAKES ABOUT 12 SERVINGS (1/8 CUP PER SERVING)

Warning: Proceed with extreme caution. These nuts can be addicting! They're delicious as an after-dinner snack, and are also a star ingredient in Prawns with Glazed Spiced Walnuts on page 87.

Canola cooking spray
2 tbsp. granulated sugar
1/4 tsp. Chinese five-spice blend (available
   in spice section of most supermarkets)

1/3 c. light corn syrup
6 oz. (170 g) walnut or pecan halves
   (about 1 1/2 c.)

1. Preheat the oven to 350° F (175° C). Coat a 9- x 9-inch baking pan or cookie sheet with canola cooking spray; set aside.
2. In a small bowl, stir together the sugar and Chinese five-spice blend; set aside.
3. Bring the corn syrup to a boil in a small nonstick saucepan over medium heat. Boil for 1 minute without stirring. Add the walnuts; stir constantly for 2–3 minutes with a wooden spoon (the nuts should be coated with the glaze). Immediately remove the saucepan from heat; sprinkle the sugar-spice mixture over the nuts and toss until the nuts are evenly coated.
4. Spread the walnuts onto the prepared pan, gently separating (as much as possible) any that are attached to each other. Bake until golden brown, about 8 minutes, being careful not to burn. Stir the nuts with a spatula, making sure the glaze is lifted up off the pan and coating the nuts well. Let cool. Serve immediately or store in an airtight container for up to 1 week.

NUTRITIONAL ANALYSES (PER SERVING)

	BEFORE	AFTER		BEFORE	AFTER
CALORIES	130	110	CHOLESTEROL	0 MG	0 MG
PROTEIN	2.2 G	2 G	FIBER	1 G	1 G
CARBOHYDRATE	6.5 G	6.5 G	SODIUM	3 MG	3 MG
FAT	12 G	8 G	% CALORIES FROM FAT	83	62
SATURATED FAT	1.5 G	0.8 G	OMEGA-3 FATTY ACIDS	1.3 G	1.2 G
MONOUNSATURATED FAT	1.8 G	1.3 G	OMEGA-6 FATTY ACIDS	6.7 G	4.7 G
POLYUNSATURATED FAT	8 G	6 G			

Pecan Almond Walnut Crunch

MAKES 10 SERVINGS (1/4 C. EACH)

Any type of nuts can be used for this recipe. I like to use pecans and almonds because they contain an impressive amount of heart-healthy monounsaturated fats.

1 c. pecan halves
1 c. whole almonds
1/2 c. walnut halves
1/2 c. sugar
1 tsp. ground cinnamon

1/8 tsp. salt
3 tbsp. fat-free half-and-half (whole milk can also be used*)
1 tsp. vanilla extract

1. If the nuts are raw (not roasted), preheat the oven to 350° F (175° C). Spread the nuts on baking sheet in a single layer. Roast for about 8 minutes, or until the nuts just begin to turn brown.
2. Stir together the sugar, cinnamon, salt, and fat-free half-and-half in a medium microwave-safe mixing bowl. Microwave on high for 3 minutes. Stir quickly (don't worry if the mixture looks like it curdled a little) and microwave on high for 3 minutes more. Stir quickly again and microwave on high for 3 minutes more or until the mixture is noticeably thick. (If you don't have a microwave, place the sugar, cinnamon, salt and fat-free half-and-half in a medium saucepan over medium heat until the mixture reaches a gentle boil. Continue to cook, stirring frequently, until mixture is noticeably thick.)
3. Stir in the vanilla extract, then add the nuts, stirring to coat the nuts well. Spoon the nuts onto waxed paper; separate with a fork. Let cool for 10 minutes. Divide into snack servings by placing 1/4-cup servings in little plastic containers or sandwich bags.

NUTRITIONAL ANALYSES (PER 1/4-C. SERVING)

	BEFORE	AFTER		BEFORE	AFTER
CALORIES	300	236	CHOLESTEROL	10 MG	0.2 MG
PROTEIN	6 G	7 G	FIBER	4 G	4 G
CARBOHYDRATE	16 G	16 G	SODIUM	64 MG	32 MG
FAT	28 G	15 G	% CALORIES FROM FAT	84	57
SATURATED FAT	4 G	1 G	OMEGA-3 FATTY ACIDS	1.2 G	0.6 G
MONOUNSATURATED FAT	10.8 G	6 G	OMEGA-6 FATTY ACIDS	8 G	4.2 G
POLYUNSATURATED FAT	9 G	6 G	*Nutritional analyses do not account for substitutions.		

Index

CONVERSION TABLES

MEASUREMENT EQUIVALENTS

1 tablespoon (tbsp) = 3 teaspoons (tsp)
1/16 cup (c) = 1 tbsp
1/8 cup = 2 tbsp
1/6 cup = 2 tbsp + 2 tsp
1/4 cup = 4 tbsp
1/3 cup = 5 tbsp + 1 tsp
3/8 cup = 6 tbsp
1/2 cup = 8 tbsp
2/3 cup = 10 tbsp + 2 tsp
3/4 cup = 12 tbsp
1 cup = 48 tsp
1 cup= 16 tbsp
8 fluid ounces (fl oz) = 1 cup
1 pint (pt) = 2 cups
1 quart (qt) = 2 pints
4 cups = 1 quart
1 gallon (gal) = 4 quarts
16 ounces (oz) = 1 pound (lb)
1 milliliter (ml) = 1 cubic centimeter (cc)
1 inch (in) = 2.54 centimeters (cm)

VOLUME CONVERSIONS

U.S. units	Canadian Metric	Australian Metric
1/4 tsp	1 mL	1 ml
1/2 tsp	2 mL	2 ml
1 tsp	5 mL	5 ml
1 tbsp	15 mL	20 ml
1/4 cup	50 ml	60 ml
1/3 cup	75 mL	80 ml
1/2 cup	125 mL	125 ml
2/3 cup	150 mL	170 ml
3/4 cup	175 mL	190 ml
1 cup	250 mL	250 ml
1 quart	1 liter	1 liter
1 1/2 quarts	1.5 liters	1.5 liters
2 quarts	2 liters	2 liters
2 1/2 quarts	2.5 liters	2.5 liters
3 quarts	3 liters	3 liters
4 quarts	4 liters	4 liters

CONVERSION TABLES

WEIGHT CONVERSIONS

U.S. units	Canadian Metric	Australian Metric
1/2 oz	15 g	15 g
1 oz	30 g	30 g
2 oz	55 g	60 g
3 oz	85 g	90 g
4 oz	115 g	125 g
8 oz	225 g	225 g
16 oz (1 lb.)	455 g	1/2 kg

OVEN TEMPERATURES

Fahrenheit	Gas Mark	Celsius
250	1/2	120
275	1	140
300	2	150
325	3	160
350	4	180
375	5	190
400	6	200
425	7	220
450	8	230
475	9	240
500	10	260

APPROXIMATE EQUIVALENTS

1 cup all-purpose pre-sifted flour = 5 oz
1 cup confectioners' sugar = 4 1/2 oz
1 cup dried beans = 6 oz
1 cup granulated sugar = 8 oz
1 cup grated cheese = 4 oz
1 cup honey/syrup = 11 oz
1 cup (packed) brown sugar = 6 oz
1 egg yolk = about 1 tbsp
1 large egg = 2 oz = about 1/4 cup
1 stick butter = 8 tbsp = 4 oz. – 1/2 cup